Escape to the great waterways outdoors

cool canals
Weekend Walks (Britain)

Phillippa Greenwood and Martine O'Callaghan

Published March 2010 by
Coolcanals Guides
128 Newtown Road
Malvern, Worcestershire
WR14 1PF
info@coolcanalsguides.com
www.coolcanalsguides.com

OUR THANKS

A huge thanks to everyone who supported us
while we were making this guidebook,
especially our families and Tufty the boat cat.

Thanks also to those who have absolutely
nothing to do with the making of this
guidebook, but who help to keep Britain's
waterways open for everyone to enjoy: The
Waterways Trust, Inland Waterways Association,
Waterway Recovery Group, The Horseboating
Society, British Waterways, all local Canal
Societies, Trusts and Associations, and all
the stalwart volunteers with their enthusiam.

OUR ETHICS & THE ENVIRONMENT

We want to inspire visitors to keep using
their waterways and help Britain's canals
stay alive. At the same time, we never
knowingly support any business or activity
not in keeping with the community, culture
and traditions that make our canals special.

Because we care about the whole earth as
well as the waterways, we 'think' green
throughout every part of the process of
making our guides: from using Ecotricity in
our office and never driving if we can walk,
to choosing eco award-winning UK printers.

Printed and bound in the UK by
Butler Tanner & Dennis, Frome, Somerset

Cool Canals is printed using 100% vegetable-based
inks on Condat Silk FSC paper, produced from
100% Elemental Chlorine Free (EFC) pulp that is
fully recyclable. It has a Forest Stewardship
Council (FSC) certification and is fully manufactured
on one site by Condat in France, an ISO14001
accredited company. All FSC certified papers are
produced by companies who support well-managed
forestry schemes which in turn actively plant and
replace trees that are cut down for pulp, typically
planting more trees than are harvested. Butler
Tanner and Dennis are also fully ISO14001 accredited
and, by both printing and binding on one site,
dramatically reduce their impact on the environment.

What's great about walking canals

Walking by water is special. Britain may be an island with windswept miles of well-loved coastal paths, but quietly inland there are over 2,000 miles of lesser known wild towpath walks. The canals of Britain humbly keep their secrets for those who care to venture on foot and follow the water.

You'll walk amongst forgotten flora and woodlands, meet wildlife, see narrowboats and breathe the balm of water in rustling green solitude; but brace yourself for the thrills of heritage and engineering wonders too.

Towpath trails are never just about walking: you're travelling back in time, treading historic trade routes that ramble defiantly through mountains, over rivers, connecting cities to the remotest countryside and passing through lock flights that climb every contour of Britain.

If you want to, you can stop off and sightsee, linger too long over lunch at a canalside pub, or hop on a boat and cheat for a bit. These water trails are so laid-back, there are no rules and nothing hurries. Every canalscape between Scotland and Cornwall is geographically different, but the water is constant, always refusing to race.

The minute you arrive you'll notice canals are naturally walker friendly: reluctant heel draggers, strollers, amblers and blister-bursting ramblers have everything in common the minute they slip their be-socked feet into boots and head off down the towpaths. Dogs can't wait for the freedom of it all and kids have the fascination of boats and water.

In summer, start early and walk till dusk, and after a walk on a winter's day, nothing beats toasting your toes over a roaring fire in the quiet hubbub of a canalside inn. Wherever you live, canals are never far away. Just pull on your boots and enjoy the great waterways outdoors!

How this book happened...
'THE GREAT CANAL WALK'

Britain's first official long-distance footpath (now called National Trails) was the Pennine Way, opened in 1965. Currently there are 18 others between Land's End and Scotland. Footpaths are recognised territory for walkers, but canal towpaths can sometimes be overlooked. Two centuries older, and around 1,400 miles longer than the longest Trail, Britain's canal network is a giant waterways' walk quietly meandering alongside these great National Trails.

Canals of Britain

The canal baggers

There are people who scramble up and down the 283 Scottish 'Munros', ticking the peaks off a list, one by one. They are called Munro baggers.

Munro-bagging wouldn't be our cup of tea – but we may be the first to officially start a new craze of canal bagging.

Join our Canalbagging Club www.canalbagging.com

We've walked the canals of Britain coast to coast and end to end from Cornwall to Scotland, following the water road through the Welsh mountains, over the Pennines, treading AONB, National Parks and brushing almost every National Trail. We've hiked across the Peak District, the Cotswolds, along the Great Glen Way, into the Lake District and even secretly sidled through London by the backdoor.

We've already collected sand in our boots on the Bude Canal, felt wind in our faces on the Caledonian and kept our bellies warmed in some characterful canalside pubs along the way... And our mission is to track down every canal in Britain.

The waterways network is a meandering maze, so there are lots of hidden branches and forgotten water trails to explore yet. But to hurry would be to miss the point. We don't carry pedometers, or care about counting miles. For us the pleasure of walking canals is enjoying the great waterways outdoors, taking time to discover places we've never walked before.

Lows are few and soon forgotten, and the highs make great entries in our guidebooks. There have been grand highs such as Pontcysyllte, Ty Newydd, Neptune's Staircase, and then more humbling highs that mean every bit as much to us, like that cuppa at Fradley, the family of swans we met in Stone, the gurning boater with elaborate stories at Stourport. The truth is any long-distance walker has moments of tedium, highs and lows. But the ferocious search for the next view around the corner keeps us going and every canal has a different story.

Our extreme towpath trek has allowed us to trespass greenest Britain, forced us to better understand urban backyards and wooed us with many forgotten wonders of historic trade routes. The canals have all been thrilling, exhausting, relaxing, frustrating and fascinating - and every step of the way, the real attraction has always been the water. We're backpacking in every season and all weathers, and plan to continue exploring until it stops being fun.

Phillippa and Martine

THE GREAT CANAL WALK
From the beach in CORNWALL to the Highlands of SCOTLAND

Introduction to this guidebook

Cool canals Weekend Walks is more than a guidebook, it's a handpicked selection of some of the greatest canal walks we've discovered through our own slow-adventures, walking all the canals of Britain from Cornwall to Scotland.

We love the freedom of the great waterways outdoors and hope to inspire you to pull on your boots to explore some of the best secrets of Britain's historic water trails.

Each walk in this guidebook is refreshingly different. Some ramble Areas of Outstanding Natural Beauty or climb mountains, others head for the sea or wander through woodlands. But don't worry, even when the landscape is dramatic and wild, towpaths are easy terrain, so every walk in this book is accessible for both experienced and new walkers.

The walks are from 2 to 12 miles. We give you all the information you need to help you plan your own waterways walking escapes. We tell you about special places and canal highlights that will spice and inform your walk. You'll find tips on the best spots to stop off for a picnic lunch, or to enjoy locally brewed real ale and tuck into some good pub food along the way.

The walk essentials are included, but nothing is prescriptive - all the water trails you'll find in this guide allow you to set your own limits, whether you want to cover the miles in one day or plan to make a weekend of it. We've included handy lists of nearby accommodation.

All this book asks is that you enjoy exploring the slow world of the waterways and submit to the peace of your own unhurried pace. These walks are for sheer pleasure.

THE WALKS

* 7 Wonders of the Waterways

Contents

Tall ships and marshes
Gloucester & Sharpness Canal - Sharpness to Saul Junction

While Horatio Nelson was fighting the Battle of Trafalgar, and Napoleon was losing at Waterloo, the Gloucester & Sharpness Canal was under construction. Legends and truths scramble romantically together on this unsung waterway which, when it opened in 1827, was the world's broadest, deepest canal. Under the guidance of Thomas Telford, it was built as a bypass from the treacherous waters of the River Severn as far as Gloucester. Since Roman times, Gloucester had been an important port, but sea-faring vessels that ventured inland too often met their end with the unpredictable sands and tides of the Severn.

With the canal's help, Gloucester became Britain's most inland port where sea vessels could come incongruously inland, flagging high sails through the rural landscape. Cargoes from around the globe arrived by sailing ship, barge, narrowboat, tanker and steamship.

During the Industrial Revolution, the canal carried grains imported to feed the hungry towns of the Midlands. And in the 20th century, it carried cocoa beans to Cadbury's factory at Frampton on Severn where they were made into chocolate crumb and then sent on narrowboats to Bournville. The canal also played an important role in the economy of the Midlands, carrying coal from the Forest of Dean.

The towpath is grassy and wide, and this walk is never claustrophobic. In most parts, the views span the river one side and canal water the other. High and low tides change the scene and, if the sun shines, you'll sing all the way. The Gloucester & Sharpness Canal lacks narrow, winding, quaint charms but makes up for it by the straightforward charisma of a waterscape riddled with history. This canal refuses to leave your imagination alone.

One of the walk's highlights is the Purton Hulks: a whispering graveyard of boats that's thought to be one of the largest clusters of historic wooden boats in the world. The first boat was dumped there in 1909. Why? A landslip between the River Severn and the Gloucester & Sharpness near Purton caused the canal to empty its water. And so, to slow down further erosion, for over half a century retired vessels were towed to the river banks and beached. They've wallowed there since in the smells of wet sand and grass, been brushed by thistles and had to listen endlessly to reeds: yet ironically, the beachings fired a fusion of life past and present, for the boats carried on beyond their graves with new purpose.

Years of tides have taken their toll on the beached wrecks, and the landscape has grown in and out of the bones of the boats. Don't just rate this as an outdoor museum of old boats: you have to walk there to know the truth. Tufts of grass sway in silence over still boat carcasses that stand like statues of soldiers in an empty battlefield. It's not eerie, but a spirit unmistakably sweeps the landscape. And whatever the weather, the wind always blows.

Every way you turn, if you look twice, the water is sending clues about the past. But it's not only heritage that makes this walk fascinating. The canal is a successful cycle of decay, regeneration, transport, industry, tourism and wildlife. This is a 'rubber neck' walk any time of year.

Look out for

Scarcely a few moments from the
thrill of Purton, the remains of the
Severn Railway Bridge add another
story to the journey. The bridge
was built in the 1870s to carry
trains over both the river and the
canal. On the towpath, you pass the
Rapunzel-calling tower that once
housed the steam engine which
created power to open the former
swing bridge. Swing bridges are a
feature of this canal as they allowed
the passage of ships with tall sails.
In 1960 two tankers, blinded by fog,
collided with one of its piers. The
bridge was later demolished and
the remains of the columns and
the unfortunate tankers can still be
spotted on the river bed at low tide.

Don't miss

You could arrive by car, park in
British Waterways' car park by the
estuary and do no more than watch
the tides come in and go back out
again. When the tides come in, the
drama is quick, but the waiting is
always wistful. It's a Turneresque
skyline with flat sand swirling in
a wash of water and the Severn
Bridge faintly in the distance.

Info about ship movements and tides.
www.gloucesterharbourtrustees.org.uk

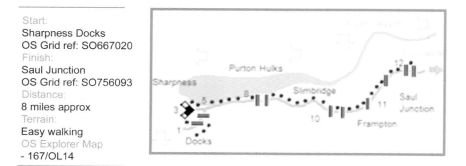

Start:
Sharpness Docks
OS Grid ref: SO667020
Finish:
Saul Junction
OS Grid ref: SO756093
Distance:
8 miles approx
Terrain:
Easy walking
OS Explorer Map
- 167/OL14

The walk - step by step

1. Start the walk from the picnic area by the huge locks leading from the River Severn into Sharpness Docks. It's worth timing it to see ships making their careful approach with the tide.

2. Follow the path to the right of the docks, along rail tracks which used to carry cargo to and from the ships.

3. After crossing the canal via the swing bridge, take the first turning right, signposted the Severn Way.

4. Take the narrow path to the left of the Vindicatrix monument and follow it until you arrive back at the water. Sharpness Rescue Station stands out with the basin on one side and the River Severn below and beyond.

5. When the water is out, the huge expanse of sand looks like the seaside but the waters of the Severn move in very quickly over this flat area.

6. Past moored boats in the marina arm, you reach a T-junction where the canal heads right to the Docks or left

towards Gloucester.

7. Follow the wide grassy towpath round to the left. Beyond the long low wall, the views stretch for miles.

8. The plaque by a round stone tower tells the story of the fate of the old Severn Railway Bridge. At low tide, you can still see some evidence of the tankers which collided with the bridge.

9. Past the first milestone, go off the towpath via one of the small paths towards the River Severn to visit the Purton Hulks 'Boat Graveyard'.

10. Two miles further on, you reach Shepherds Patch, where there's a chance to stop for a cuppa or a pint, or visit Slimbridge Wetland Centre.

11. To detour through the pretty village of Frampton on Severn, take the road or cross the field by Splatt Bridge.

12. Back on the towpath at Fretherne Bridge, follow the towpath towards the busy hub of Saul Junction where the restoration of the Cotswold Canals will one day reopen a link to the Thames.

Where to eat

Pier View Hotel
Sharpness. Overlooks docks. T:01453 811255

Tudor Arms
Shepherds Patch. Canalside by Patch Bridge.
T:01453 890306 www.thetudorarms.co.uk

Slimbridge Boat Station Café (the Black Shed)
Nr.Slimbridge. Canalside near Patch Bridge.
T:01453 899190 / 07547 829035

The Three Horseshoes
Frampton on Severn. In the village, a short
walk from Splatt Bridge. T:01452 740463

The Bell Inn
Frampton on Severn. On the village green, a
short walk from Fretherne Bridge.
T:01452 740346 www.thebellatframpton.co.uk

The Stables Café
Saul Junction. Canalside by Sandfield Bridge.
Open daily 0900-1630 (Mondays from 1000)
T:01452 741965 www.thestablescafe.co.uk

Ship Inn
Framilode. Canalside on the disused
Stroudwater Canal near Saul Junction. Rooms
T:01452 740260

Best picnic spot
On the banks of the canal near Patch Bridge

Sharpness Docks
The start of the walk is coincidentally also
the start of the Severn Way. The docks are
blunt and not meant for tourists but that
adds to the fascination. Old tram rails hide
in the grass, chunky chains coil and rust,
and what's not functional is ignored.

Bike hire
Slimbridge Boat Station. Canalside near
Patch Bridge.
T:01453 899190 / 07547 829035

Where to stay

Canalside B&Bs
Frampton Court Estate
Frampton on Severn. Short
walk from Fretherne Bridge.
T:01452 740698
www.framptoncourtestate.co.uk
The True Heart
Frampton on Severn. Short
walk from canal. T:01452
740504 www.thetrueheart.co.uk
Tythe House
Frampton on Severn. A short
walk from Splatt Bridge.
T:01452 740270
www.tythehousebandb.co.uk

Canalside campsites
Tudor Caravan Park 4-pennant
(David Bellamy Conservation
Award - Gold) Shepherds
Patch. Canalside by Patch
Bridge. T:01453 890483
www.tudorcaravanpark.co.uk

Canalside cottages
The Orangery, Frampton Court
Estate (see B&Bs)
Tanhouse Farm Cottages 5-star
Frampton on Severn. Short
walk from Splatt Bridge
T:01452 741072
www.tanhouse-farm.co.uk

Canalside pubs & Inns
Tudor Arms Lodge, Shepherds
Patch. Short walk from Patch
Bridge T:01453 890306
www.thetudorarms.co.uk
The Bell Inn 4-star
Frampton on Severn. Short
walk from Fretherne Bridge.
T:01452 740346
www.thebellatframpton.co.uk

And more
Good choice of self-catering,
B&B and hotels in the area.
www.cotswolds.com

How to get there

Train info
Nearest train station is Cam & Dursley
National Rail Enquiries T:08457 484950
Bus info
Traveline T:0871 2002233
Parking
British Waterways car park in docks (charge)

Local Tourist info

Gloucester Tourist Information Centre
T:01452 396572 www.cotswolds.com
Cotswold Canals Trust
Working to restore the Stroudwater Navigation
and Thames & Severn Canal.
T:01285 643440 www.cotswoldcanals.com
Saul Junction Heritage Centre
The centre is run by volunteers and aims
to inform visitors about the history of the
Stroudwater and Thames & Severn Canals,
and the purpose of re-establishing a navigable
link to the Thames. Open Sat, Sun, Bank Hols.
T:01285 643440 www.cotswoldcanals.com
Slimbridge Wildfowl & Wetlands Trust
The birthplace of modern conservation &
home of the Wildfowl & Wetlands Trust attracts
thousands of ducks, geese and swans every
year, as well as rarer species of flora and
fauna. T:01453 891900 www.wwt.org.uk
Friends of Purton
Hope to secure the future of the Purton Hulks
T:07833 143231 www.friendsofpurton.org.uk

Boats

Glevum Boat Hire
Slimbridge Boat Station. Day boat hire.
T:01453 899190
Cotswold Canals Trust Boat Trips
Saul Junction. Short cruises on
'Perseverance'. Saturdays, Sundays & Bank
Holiday Mondays only, April to September.
T:01285 643440 www.cotswoldcanals.com

The famous 16
Kennet & Avon Canal - Caen Hill & Devizes

Do hill walks come better than this? Wiltshire wafts its magic to bulk 29 locks into just over two short miles from Lower Foxhangers Bridge to Devizes along the Kennet & Avon Canal.

Halfway through the locks, the canal climbs to its highlight at the 16-lock Caen Hill Flight, one of the official Seven Wonders of Britain's canals. The lock arms individually are arguably not as aesthetically pleasing as the great wooden beams on narrow canals such as the Worcester & Birmingham Canal or the Staffordshire & Worcestershire, but the panorama of these humungous black and white wings concertinaing up the hillside make a spectacle that is guaranteed to stay in your mind long after you hang up your boots at the end of the walk.

Don't worry that you'll need beefy calf muscles or expensive walking poles; you'll barely notice the incline as high thoughts will carry your feet effortlessly along the well-maintained towpath. Despite the easy walking, it's a good idea to allow extra time because, as well as the obvious attractions of the trail, there are other temptations to distract you too.

If the lure of the teashop beckoning like a gingerbread house in the woods at the top of the flight doesn't get you, the sight of barrels stacked on the canalside just beyond it will. Wadsworth Brewery invites you in to tour and taste, and who in their right mind could refuse?

Then when you reach Devizes, the ever-active Kennet & Avon Canal Trust welcome you with their packed small shop and museum, and there's always time for an ice cream if you want.

The Kennet & Avon Canal hasn't always been an idyllic trail for walkers. It's only thanks to the colossal efforts of the Kennet & Avon Canal Trust and others that the canal has survived its turbulent past. 200 years ago, the canal began as a busy trade route, until competition from the railways forced the canal to close. The ironic trick of the railway was that it was even cheeky enough to use canal boats to transport the materials it needed to build its rail tracks! The Kennet & Avon was eventually reopened by the Queen in 1990 for leisure boating.

The success of the canal and fame of the Caen Hill Flight along with the attraction of its leafy canalscape mean this isn't one of Britain's secret undiscovered canal trails. Expect to scuff past towpath amblers and trekkers and, because it's part of Sustrans' National Cycle Network (Route 4 joins the canal at Devizes and follows the canal all the way to Bath), it's popular with cyclists too.

And of course there are boats. You'll probably pass the same boats on your way back up the flight as when you walked down it - it takes them a lot longer to work through all those locks than it does for you to walk past!

If you want the place all to yourself, it's best to go in the depths of winter, on a midweek morning when there's been a very bad weather forecast. But whether you like walking in a crowd or alone, with a summer picnic or winter waterproofs - the Caen Hill Flight is determined to be the highlight.

FUNDRAISERS' LOCK
IN RECOGNITION OF MANY YEARS OF
DEVOTED FUND-RAISING WORK BY
CANAL TRUST MEMBERS AND OTHERS

KENNET & AVON CANAL
1794 - 1804

Caen Hill Locks
via Subway

4

Highlight of the walk

The 16 locks known as the Caen Hill Flight are actually part of a much longer stretch of 29 locks spread over about 2¼ miles leading to Devizes. Built by engineer John Rennie, the 29 locks carry boats a total of 237ft up the steep hill to Devizes. Boaters travelling through the flight have to arrive between set times and, as there is no mooring allowed up the flight, they must complete all 16 locks in time. The Caen Hill Flight is also one of the Seven Wonders of the Waterways.

Did you know?

The Devizes to Westminster International Canoe Race (the longest nonstop canoe race in the world) sets off from Devizes Wharf. The race covers 125 miles to Westminster Bridge in London (52 miles on the Kennet & Avon Canal, 55 miles on the River Thames and a final stretch on the tidal Thames).

T:0118 9665912 www.dwrace.org.uk

Look out for

There are several locks up the flight named after volunteers from the Kennet & Avon Canal Trust who worked so hard to achieve the successful restoration of this canal.

Start & Finish:
Caen Hill Locks
OS Grid ref: ST986615
Distance:
5 miles approx (circular)
Terrain:
Easy walking though hilly
on the return walk up the
lock flight
OS Explorer Map
- 156/157

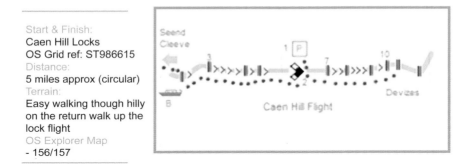

The walk - step by step

1. Start the walk at the conveniently placed car park near the top of the Caen Hill Flight.

2. Cross the picnic area then the locks and turn right to follow the flight downhill, with open views of the countryside ahead of you.

3. At the bottom of the flight, follow the towpath under the road.

4. At lock 23, there's a sign to the left for Lower Foxhangers Farm. After a quick peep at the boatyard beyond, turn round and walk back towards the locks from a different direction (or continue along the towpath to Seend Cleeve or Sells Green for a pub lunch)

5. The Caen Hill Flight's 16 locks look even more dramatic (or daunting to boaters) from this perspective, winging their way up the hill.

6. Most locks have signs giving them special names to commemorate

individuals or groups who have supported the Kennet & Avon Canal Trust's efforts to restore the canal and maintain it for the future.

7. At the top of the flight, next to lock 44, Caen Hill Café is the perfect chance for a cuppa and cake, sitting on the terrace overlooking the locks and the surrounding countryside.

8. Beyond the café, the towpath continues past boat moorings on the opposite side of the canal, under a bridge then past another couple of locks (with a pub between).

9. Cross to the other side of the canal just beyond the main road into Devizes. There are moored boats and a glimpse of beer barrels stacked outside Wadworth's Brewery opposite.

10. Cross over the canal at bridge 140 to reach the wharf and the Kennet & Avon Canal Trust's Museum and Shop. After you've finished exploring, simply retrace your footsteps back to the car park by the locks.

Where to eat

Caen Hill Café
Devizes. Canalside overlooking Caen Hill Locks (by lock 44). Open daily 1000-1700. T:01452 318000

Black Horse Pub
Devizes. Canalside between locks 47 & 48. T:01380 723930

Three Magpies
Sells Green. Short walk from bridge 149. T:01380 828389 www.threemagpies.co.uk

Barge Inn
Seend Cleeve. Canalside by lock no.19, a couple of miles beyond the boatyard T:01380 828230 www.bargeinnseend.co.uk

Best picnic spot
Designated picnic area alongside the locks

Devizes
Choice of other pubs and cafés in Devizes

Wadworth Brewery Visitor Centre & Shop
Wadworth's, founded in 1875 in Devizes, is still run as a family business by the family of Wadworth's business partner. The Victorian brewery is well known not only for its beer but also for its shire horses, whose stables are open to the public. The Visitor Centre has an interesting small exhibition and shop. Open Mon-Fri 1000-1730, Sat 1000-1600. Free admission. Guided tours of the brewery twice daily (Charge for the tours). T:01380 732277 www.wadworth.co.uk

The Wharf Theatre, Devizes
96-seat theatre in former canal warehouse, entirely run by volunteers. There is also a youth theatre which runs a range of workshops, and the theatre is available for private hire. T:01380 724741 www.wharftheatre.co.uk

Where to stay

Canalside B&Bs
Lower Foxhangers Farm
Lower Foxhangers Farm (See Cottages for details)
Rockley House
Devizes. Canalside near bridge 138. T:01380 724090
www.rockleyhouse.com
Rosemundy Cottage 4-star (Green Tourism Silver Award)
Devizes. Canalside near bridge 137. T:01380 727122
www.rosemundycottage.co.uk

Canalside campsites
Lower Foxhangers Farm (See Cottages for details)
Devizes Camping & Caravanning Club Site
Canalside behind The Three Magpies near bridge 149. T:01380 828839
campingandcaravanningclub.co.uk

Canalside cottages
Dairy House & Hayloft
Rowde. Canalside by Caen Hill Flight. T:01380 728883
www.canalbarn.co.uk
Lower Foxhangers Farm
Devizes. Near canal by lock 23. Mobile holiday homes. T:01380 828254
www.foxhangers.com

Canalside pubs & inns
George & Dragon 4-star
Rowde. A short walk from Caen Hill Locks.
T:01380 723053
thegeorgeanddragonrowde.co.uk

And more
Good choice of self-catering, B&B and hotel accommodation in and around Devizes.
www.visitwiltshire.co.uk

How to get there

Train info
Nearest train station is Melksham
National Rail Enquiries T:08457 484950
Bus info
Traveline T:0871 2002233
Parking
Car park by the lock flight (charge)

Local Tourist info

Devizes Tourist Information Centre
T:01380 729408 www.visitwiltshire.co.uk
Kennet & Avon Canal Trust
The Trust, based in Devizes (with other branches along the entire canal) has worked tirelessly for over 40 years. Initially formed to bring about the restoration of the Kennet & Avon, its main objectives now are to continue to protect, enhance and promote the canal.
T:01380 721279 www.katrust.org.uk
Kennet & Avon Canal Museum & Shop
Devizes. Run and staffed by the K&A Canal Trust, the small museum is above the well-stocked shop, and gives an insight into the Kennet & Avon Canal from inception to restoration. Open at the same time as the shop, usually 1000-1700 March to November, 1000-1600 rest of the year. Small admission charge to the museum.
T:01380 729489

Boats

Foxhangers Canal Holidays
Rowde, Devizes. Holiday boat hire.
T:01380 828795
White Horse Boats
Devizes Wharf. Holiday boat hire. Also trip boat operates weekends from Easter to end September. T:01380 728504
www.whitehorseboats.co.uk

The Oxford Canal travels 77 almost uninterrupted rural miles between two cities. Water nonchalantly connects Oxford at one end of the canal to Coventry at the other. Both cities can brag claims to fame: one is applauded for its donnishness, and the other less cerebrally celebrated for nude horse riding.

Along the quiet southerly section of this canal, a four-mile stretch from Pigeon Bridge to Lower Heyford makes a perfect leisurely amble. Because the route is easy walking and relatively flat, it's also unspectacular for canal engineering marvels; yet instead, you tread through opulent greenery in an unspoilt waterways landscape worth every step you pace.

This is real country walking. Between manure wafts and summer sounds of birds twittering, you might hear occasional deeper bouts of rural gunshots and game squawks. The River Cherwell follows the canal most of the way and the local railway line hoots not far away.

The M40 will temporarily tamper with the canal's solitude much further north, but luckily on this more southerly walk, there's a noticeable absence of even minor roads so noise pollution never spoils the ambience.

On a lazy sunny day ambling along this towpath, it's hard to imagine that the Oxford Canal was originally part of a busy major freight route between London and the Midlands. It was the arrival of the wider and speedier Grand Union Canal during the heyday of the Industrial Revolution that changed the fate of the Oxford, and probably helped shape it into today's modest canal unbothered by progress.

Stone bridges still arc the water reflecting local Cotswold colours, and little has been built beyond to disturb the peace and quiet. This walk probably feels more remote than it actually is, and that makes it a deceptively accessible great escape on foot for a day.

Why pick these four miles, when there's the possibility of even prettier walks further each way on the Oxford Canal? Well, this stretch is not only a delicious rural trail, there's the surprise bonus of a fab teashop treat at both ends of the walk too. It's worth getting up extra early to make sure you have plenty of time for both. Walks rarely get more satisfying.

An Oxford brew near the city, yet far away, in a waterside tearoom with everything: scones, cream, Earl Grey tea and more charm than you can drink all in one go. On a sleepy leafy stretch of the Oxford Canal, you'll find Pan the narrowboat moored alongside its own smallholding that's a farmshop and idyllic canalside tearoom too. It's organic, with happy free-range hens, waterside seating and cupfuls of character. And at the other end of this rural walk, drink tea and gongoozle at Kizzie's Bar amidst the hustle and bustle of the boatyard of Lower Heyford.

Can England get any better than a pot of tea, a wedge of Victoria sponge and an unhurried waterside tramp along the Oxford Canal?

British Waterways

Dashwoods Lock

Highlight of the walk

Dashwood Lock is set in open countryside, seemingly in the middle of nowhere. This is a great spot for a picnic - there's a bench alongside the lock, with 360-degree views along the canal and over open fields full of munching cattle.

Did you know?

The entire length of the Oxford Canal, from Oxford to Coventry, is a designated waymarked path - the Oxford Canal Walk. The walk connects the two cathedral cities of Oxford and Coventry, and follows such a rural course that it only crosses one road.

Fascinating fact

The Oxford Canal was one of the first canals built and is one of the most rural in the country. The southern part of the canal winds gently through fields and the occasional village. One of its features is the prevalence of woooden black and white lift bridges, used by farmers to access their land. The bridges are normally left down over the canal so boaters need to lift them up (a surprisingly simple process) for their boats to pass underneath.

Start:
Pigeon Lock
OS Grid ref: SP486193
Finish:
Heyford Wharf
OS Grid ref: SP483247
Distance:
4 miles (5 from Tackley)
Terrain:
Flat easy walking. Can be muddy in rural parts after rain.
OS Explorer Map - 180

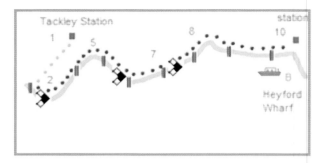

The walk - step by step

1. If you start the walk at Tackley station (just under a mile from the canal), the path crosses Akeman Street, an old Roman road.

2. Follow Oxfordshire Way signs for a short while before reaching Pigeon Lock (the Way carries on into the village of Kirtlington).

3. Turn left onto the towpath and head past the lock.

4. Continuing northwards, the canal is lined by trees on both sides, with some glimpses on the opposite bank of a woodland trail leading to a clearing. It seems a popular picnic spot for day hireboats.

5. The trees start to thin out between bridges 212 and 211 as the surrounding farmland becomes more visible on the approach to shady Northbrook Lock, the first of two locks on this stretch of canal.

6. Just beyond the lock, the River Cherwell is very much evident as an old Cotswold stone packhorse bridge crosses the river alongside bridge 210 over the canal. There is a pretty thatched cottage on the other bank.

7. Straight open approach to the perfectly situated Dashwood Lock with open views all around.

8. Just beyond bridge 208, the river and railway rejoin the canal as it heads past the grounds of Rousham House and Gardens.

9. A line of moored boats on the approach between bridge 207 and the railway bridge marks the approach to Lower Heyford, before bursting into a hub of activity and life around Heyford Wharf overlooking a basin full of holiday and day hireboats.

10. The railway station is right next to the canal at this point, making for an easy return to Tackley or Oxford, or further northwards to Banbury.

Where to eat

Floating Farm Shop
Kirtlington. Canalside above Pigeon Lock. Teas and snacks on Sundays 1000-1730, March to December. It's worth timing your walk to fit with its opening hours as, from the other side of the canal, you'll be enticed by evocatively laid tables at the waterside and the promise of home-grown produce from Pan, the narrowboat moored next to the smallholding. T:07837 362683

Oxford Arms
Kirtlington. In the village, about a mile from the canal. T:01869 350208 www.oxford-arms.co.uk

Dashwood Hotel & Restaurant
Kirtlington. About a mile from the canal. T:01869 352707 www.thedashwood.co.uk

Kizzie's Waterside Bar & Bistro
Lower Heyford. Canalside in the wharf. Enjoy tea, cake and a spot of gongoozling. Open daily 0900-1700. Weekends 1000-1500 in winter. T:01869 340348 www.oxfordshire-narrowboats.co.uk

The Bell Inn
Lower Heyford. A short walk from the canal. T:01869 347176

Best picnic spot
By Dashwood Lock

James Brindley
The twists and turns of the Oxford Canal are characteristic of its engineer James Brindley. He preferred to follow the land's contours and go round, rather than over or through, any obstacles. Other engineers, such as Thomas Telford, had other ideas, building long tunnels, challenging lock flights and great aqueducts.

Where to stay

Canalside B&Bs
The Colliers 3-diamond Tackley. A short walk from the canal. Dogs (and horses!) welcome. T:01869 331255 www.colliersbnb.co.uk

Canalside campsites
Heyford Leys Camping Park Upper Heyford. About a mile from the canal. T:01869 232048 www.heyfordleyspark.co.uk

Canalside hotels
Dashwood Hotel & Restaurant Kirtlington. About a mile from the canal. T:01869 352707 www.thedashwood.co.uk

Holt Hotel 3-star Steeple Aston. Approx a mile from Lower Heyford. T:01869 340259 www.holthotel-oxford.co.uk

And more
There's also a good choice of self-catering, B&B and hotel accommodation in and around nearby Steeple Aston, Middle Aston and Oxford. www.visitoxford.org

How to get there

Train info

Tackley (short distance from start of walk) &
Lower Heyford (canalside at end of walk)
National Rail Enquiries T:08457 484950

Bus info

Traveline T:0871 2002233

Parking

Roadside in the village or at one of the train
stations

Local Tourist info

Oxford Tourist Information Centre

T:01865 252200 www.visitoxford.org/tic

Rousham House and Gardens

Rousham House is still in the ownership of the
same family it was built for in 1635 and the
landscape gardens by William Kent (1685-
1748) remain almost as they were set out
originally for the house. The House is only
open by prior arrangement, but the Gardens
open daily 1000-1800 or dusk (last admission
1630). Admission charge (no dogs allowed in
the Gardens). No tearoom so take a picnic.
T:01869 347110 www.rousham.org

Boats

Oxfordshire Narrowboats

Lower Heyford. Holiday and day boat hire. The
day boats are also available for private charter,
complete with skipper and food. Bike hire is
also available from the boat yard.
T:01869 340348
www.oxfordshire-narrowboats.co.uk

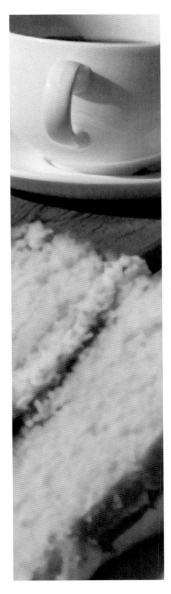

Seagulls and sails

An estuary wind dusts your lips with salt and you sense the Exeter Ship Canal pays no homage to quaint narrowboats and their folkie roses and castles. This is a canal with a different character to those narrow, bendy, cruising rings that charm holiday boaters. Exeter's canal has sea-bound history on a waterway that runs from the city to the River Exe estuary.

In the late 1200s the River Exe was navigable and helped make Exeter a busy port. But by the 1500s the river was doomed as a trade route after a collision of extortionate tolls and over-silting (caused by weirs built to harbour power for the woollen mills) which rendered the water virtually impassable.

To provide a new route, the Exeter Ship Canal was opened in 1567 - an amazing two centuries before Telford and Brindley, the great engineers responsible for Britain's era of canal mania, were even born. Britain's canals mostly served the Industrial Revolution, yet the Exeter Canal was so ahead of its time, Mary Queen of Scots was still bickering with Elizabeth 1 whilst the first sod of earth was being dug out of the ground for this pioneering canal.

Bags of heritage and Tudor dramas of wooden ships could milk their stories along this ancient trade route. But nostalgia is politely dusted aside by an up-to-the-minute canal that's alive and well, busy enjoying the great waterways outdoors with bikes, boots, boat paddles and frenetically happy dogs every way you turn.

Admittedly, we quiet canal walkers don't often cherish the thought of sharing a towpath with hoards of over-enthusiastic cyclists, but the towpath on the Exeter Ship Canal is wide enough to accommodate both slow boots and speedier saddles. And walking couldn't be easier than this: with a flat, hard-surfaced path most of the way. Look out for a tiny Tom Sawyer-style gate painted white. Only boots are allowed beyond this gate onto a tighter path that lets a walker own the space.

Traffic noise only disturbs the walk in parts and mostly sweet sounds travel the water, with sea birds calling over jangling anchors and the beating flaps of sails. Masts soar over the flat windswept landscape and rustling reeds lining the water's edge can only point in one direction, away from the sea.

One of the popular reasons people flock to the Exeter Ship Canal is its waterside pubs. The Double Locks and the Turf are two of the best pubs anywhere on Britain's canal networks (and possibly the most dog-friendly). In summer there's the temptation of supreme beer gardens calling from both pubs along the route and the weak-willed are bound to end up stopping twice. And when the season makes the canal chilly, lunch in a cosy pub warming your toes over an open fire makes sense.

Whatever time of year you walk the Exeter, it's a wild walk comfortably tamed by the easy terrain of the well-kept towpath. Heritage, wildlife, big boats, canoes, whiffs of the sea and good pubs into the bargain: the Exeter Ship Canal makes an exhilarating walk.

Butt's Ferry

TIS 'ER YOU CATCH THE FERRY
A FUNNY BOAT IT BE . . .
BUT IT GETS YOU ACROSS THE
RIVER FOR ONLY 30p
(CHILD 20p)

11am-5pm EAST

Highlight of the walk

The Double Lock - the Exeter Ship Canal was the first canal in Britain to have pound locks (where water fills the lock from a 'pound' or reservoir to the side of the lock). The double lock was built in the late 1600s to replace a trio of locks. It was so unusually large that small boats were carried round the lock on rail tracks to save the water, time and effort needed to fill the lock.

Did you know?

Exeter Ship Canal is part of the Exe Valley Way, a long-distance trail covering 50 miles northwards from Starcross to the village of Exford on Exmoor. Its entire length is also part of National Route 2 of the National Cycle Network.

Fascinating fact

Most canals are built with just one towpath but, uniquely, the Exeter Ship Canal has one on each side of the water. This meant that two working horses at a time could be used to pull larger, heavier boats. The dual towpaths run as far as the now disused Topsham Lock, with the final stretch to Turf Lock having a towpath just on the one side of the canal.

Start:
Exeter Quayside
OS Grid ref: SX920920
Finish:
Turf Lock
OS Grid ref: SX963860
Distance:
5¼ miles approx
Terrain:
Easy walking
OS Explorer Map
- 114/110

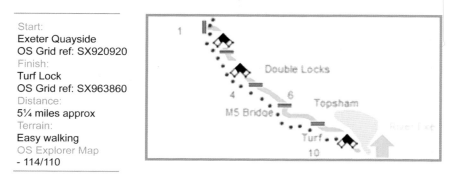

The walk - step by step

1. From the quayside, it's possible to take the towpath on either side of the canal as far as the now disused Topsham Lock. Cross the pedestrian bridge by the quay to take the path on the right-hand side of the canal.

2. Pass Kings Arms Sluice and moored boats in the basin, then head south.

3. On the opposite bank, the Riverside Valley Park flanks the canal all the way down towards the Double Lock.

4. A short distance beyond the lock, Countess Wear moving bridge carries the main road across the canal. Climb the steps up to the road to cross at the pedestrian crossing, and then continue along the towpath beyond.

5. The canal widens as it passes the site of the old limekilns where ships waited for high tides and good weather to join the estuary at the original entrance to the canal.

6. Noise of the road is now unavoidable as you walk under the M5 flyover, but peace soon returns.

7. The towpath splits into two sections with walkers going through a gate to the narrower, more over-grown path by the canal, while cyclists are directed to the right.

8. Topsham, with its sailing boats, is visible across the canal and estuary as you reach the pedestrian swing bridge and lock-keeper's cottage at the site of the original Topsham Lock. (Cross the bridge if you want to catch the ferry, which has operated for generations, across the estuary).

9. Open views, over Exminster Marshes Nature Reserve to your right, and the canal with estuary beyond to your left, continue for 1½ miles.

10. The end of the canal is marked by the dramatic setting of Turf Lock, where you can shorten your return journey by catching a ferry across the estuary back to Topsham.

Where to eat

The Double Locks pub

As its name suggests, the pub overlooks the canal's notorious double lock a mile and a bit from Exeter Quay. Dogs welcome.
T:01392 256947 www.doublelocks.com

The Turf pub

By Turf Lock. One of only a few pubs in the UK which can't be reached by car (nearest parking ½-mile). Dogs welcome.
T:01392 833128 www.turfpub.net

The Swan's Nest

Exminster. About half a mile from pedestrian bridge at original site of Topsham Lock.
T:01392 832371 www.swans-nest.co.uk

Route 2 Eco Café Bar

Topsham. A short walk from Topsham Ferry. Eco-friendly. Bike hire. T:01392 875085

Best picnic spot

Overlooking estuary by Turf Lock

Quayside

Large choice of pubs and cafés along the quayside in Exeter.

Canoe and bike hire

Exeter quayside. All types of bikes including tandems, child bikes & child seats. Single and double kayaks, open Canadian canoes. Bike shop & hire centre open daily all year.
T:01392 424241 www.saddlepaddle.co.uk

Canoe trips

Full or half day canoe trips along the canal including some basic bush craft lessons
T:01395 200522
www.essential-adventure.co.uk

Where to stay

Canalside campsites

The Turf
By Turf Lock. Wild camping with the benefits of a pub on tap! Ask at the bar (or phone for details) and you can usually pitch your tent in the pub garden perched on the water's edge between the estuary and the canal.
T:01392 833128
www.turfpub.net

Canalside cottages

Topsham Lock Cottage, Topsham. By swing bridge. Ideal for groups or visitors interested in the natural environment of the estuary.
T:01392 219600
www.topshamlockcottage.co.uk

Steam Packet Apartments Topsham. A short walk from the Topsham Ferry. Above Route 2 Café, serviced by Globe Hotel.
T:01392 873471
www.route2topsham.co.uk

Canalside hotels

The Globe Hotel 2-star Topsham. A short walk from the Topsham Ferry. Green Tourism Awards. Dog-friendly. Wheelchair access.
T:01392 873471
www.globehotel.com

And more

There's also a good choice of self-catering, B&B and hotel accommodation in and around Exeter, Topsham & Exmouth.
www.exeter.gov.uk

How to get there

Train info

Exeter St Thomas, Exeter Central, Exeter St Davids & Starcross (approx 2 miles from Turf) National Rail Enquiries T:08457 484950

Bus info

Traveline T:0871 2002233

Parking

Car park near quayside (charge) or roadside

Local Tourist info

Quay House Visitor Centre

T:01392 271611 www.exeter.gov.uk

Boats & ferries

Butt's Pull Ferry

Exeter. Crosses river at the quayside (has operated since at least 1641). Daily Easter to October, 1100-1700, & weekends for the rest of the year, depending on the weather.

'Kingsley'

Hourly cruises from quayside to Double Locks pub. Daily June, July & August. Weekends & bank hols only in April, May & September. Also available for private charter.
T:07984 368442 www.exetercruises.com

Topsham Turf Ferry

Topsham to Turf. Daily Easter hols & from late May to mid September, weekends April, rest of May & September. Available for private charter.
T:07778 370582 www.topshamtoturfferry.co.uk

Topsham Ferry

Topsham to canal T:07801 203338

The White Heather

Ferry from Double Lock to Turf Lock, 3 times a day. T:07806 554093

Stuart Line Cruises

River cruises from Topsham and limited special cruises along the Exeter Ship Canal.
T:01395 222144 www.stuartlinecruises.co.uk

Any city canal can be a beautiful warts-and-all walk, yet the Regent's Canal tiptoes through England's capital city and still manages to quietly surprise the walker with its slow secrets. This is a city walk through the backdoor, catching London in private, with its slippers on.

The canal sets off from the well-off residential patch around Little Venice, with tree-lined roads bordering the gentle water. Here, the canal is eloquently loved. Moored boats that line the water's edge are made into narrow-homes, and other boats take tourists out for a ride. The zone is in keeping with the romance of its name. However, Little Venice risks the wrath of Birmingham for stealing the Italian connection, since Birmingham is the official capital of the canals with more waterways than the real Venice.

Follow the towpath beyond the whitewashed haven of Little Venice and more intrigue unfolds. The big city has two tales to tell - there's the one it intends you to hear, and then the quieter view from the water. It soon becomes impossible to position yourself with the 'other' London as it disapears from any of the senses. The 4-mph water-zone doesn't let anything infringe the simplicity.

Before the M1 was a twinkle in the industrialists' eye, the canals had already linked London to the rest of Britain for more than a century. The canal was first opened in 1820 and named after the Prince Regent, later to be King George IV. London, naturally, is rife with royal connections. The canal even treads on land that was once the hunting grounds of Henry VIII (until in 1811 John Nash landscaped them into the Royal Park).

Regency housing backing onto the canal isn't the whole story of this walk. The canal briefly gets tangled up into patches of urban bleakness but the water always keeps the mood sweet and opens up again into urban leafiness and clean-cut stretches.

Be prepared for tropical squawking, tusks and unmentionable aromas to surprise you, as the towpath walks straight through the middle of London Zoo. (There's mesh to keep you safe!)

On another turn in the water, multi-coloured tie-dyed Camden is the compulsory cool bit of the walk. The markets are world famous for joss-stick accessories and possibly more purple-patterned trousers than anywhere else on earth. Even outdoor-minded walkers who are shop-phobics might be tempted to stalk the markets for bargains of zappy-labelled clothes or not-over-packaged earthy veg.

The Regent's Canal is a different experience to walking those cosier narrow canals of the Midlands or the North, and the towpaths are fastidiously hard-surfaced with less appeal than soft grass paths, yet the waterways' balm manages to bring out the same old-fashioned smiles and hellos that canals have a knack of doing - even when it takes you into the concrete heart of the capital.

An urban walk into the most secret side of the capital city.

British
Waterways
London

'Blow up' Bri

Puppet
Theatre
Barge

Art Gallery/
ook

Rose

Little Ve

Waterside
afé/The Floating
oater Office

Londo
Water
Comp

Y

Highlight of the walk

The towpath runs alongside Regent's Park. John Nash, the designer of both the canal and Regent's Park, had intended the canal to run through the middle of the park. But he was convinced by others that the delicate residents of the park would be horrified by the foul language used by navvies building the canal, so in the end, he decided to take the canal round the edge instead. Not too bad a compromise!

Did you know?

The poet, Robert Browning, used to live in a house overlooking the Regent's Canal. Having compared the canal to Venice, he is thought to be the first person to name the area Little Venice. The small island in the middle of the Pool of Little Venice is called Browning's Island after him.

Fascinating fact

Camden Lock is the name for the area around the locks and markets at Camden yet there is no Camden Lock. The twin locks at the centre of Camden are actually called Hampstead Road Lock.

Start:
Little Venice
OS Grid ref: TQ262818
Finish:
Camden Lock
OS Grid ref: TQ288841
Distance:
2 miles approx
Terrain:
Flat easy walking.
OS Explorer Map - 173
(or London A-Z)

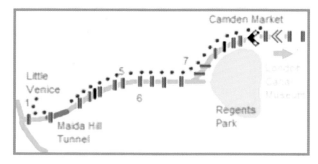

The walk - step by step

1. The pool of Little Venice makes a grand start to the walk. This wide open space is lined with boats and surrounded by white stucco-clad Regency houses.

2. Take the towpath under Warwick Avenue Bridge. The scene ahead is of moored boats on both sides of the water, mirrored by the terraces of Regency houses. Some residential boat owners have developed their canalside gardens to such an extent, it is a haven of pots and wisteria.

3. Follow the road alongside and, just beyond the moorings by Maida Hill Tunnel, cross the road to Aberdeen Place. Carry on until you pass Crocker's Folly pub on your left, then straight along the path (signposted Regent's Canal) to rejoin the towpath down steep steps at the other end.

4. Continuing under the next couple of busy road and rail bridges, you enter a scene of tranquillity - white mansions line the opposite side of the canal, their gardens and weeping willows swooping down to the water. This is the edge of Regent's Park.

5. Look out for the aptly named 'Blow Up Bridge' - a boat with a cargo of gunpowder bound for the Midlands exploded here in 1874, demolishing the existing bridge and terrifying the residents. When rebuilt, the pillars were turned round, so there are now rope grooves on both sides.

6. Just beyond the bridge, notice the cages and wire as the canal goes through part of London Zoo - watch for Red River hogs, the giraffe house and a huge aviary of exotic birds.

7. Past Cumberland Basin, with its moored boats and unusual Chinese restaurant, the canal curves under a quick succession of low road and rail bridges before arriving at the hustle and bustle of Camden. (If you follow the towpath for another mile, you'll reach Battlebridge Basin and the London Canal Museum)

Where to eat

Boat House
Canalside at Little Venice.
T:0207 2866752 www.boathouselondon.co.uk

The Waterway
Canalside at Little Venice.
T:0207 2663557 www.thewaterway.co.uk

The Bridge House & Canal Café Theatre
Canalside at Little Venice.
T:0207 2664326 www.canalcafetheatre.com

Waterside Café
Moored in Little Venice. T:0207 2661066

Café Laville
Perched on top of Maida Hill Tunnel,
overlooking the canal.
T:0207 7062620

Feng Shang Princess
Floating Chinese restaurant boat moored in
Cumberland Basin.
T:0207 4858137 / 0216 www.fengshang.co.uk

Lock 17
Canalside by Camden Lock.
T:0207 4285929 www.lock17-camden.co.uk

Starbucks Coffee Company
In the old Lock Keeper's Cottage. Canalside
overlooking Camden Lock.
T:0207 4851986 www.starbucks.co.uk

The Ice Wharf
Canalside by Camden Lock.
T:0207 4283770 www.jdwetherspoon.co.uk

The Constitution
Canalside by St Pancras Way Bridge, just
beyond Camden.
T:0207 3874805

Best picnic spot
At Little Venice or alongside Regent's Park.

And more
Large choice of other pubs and cafés in and
around the route from Little Venice to Camden.

Where to stay

Canalside cottages
Europa House Apartments
Little Venice. Serviced
apartments, a short walk from
the canal.
T:0207 7245924
europahouseapartments.co.uk

Canalside hotels
The Colonnade Hotel 4-star
Little Venice. Short walk from
the canal.
T:0207 2861052
www.theetoncollection.com

Holiday Inn Camden Lock
4-star. Canalside by Camden
Lock. Wheelchair access.
T:0207 4854343
www.holidayinncamden.co.uk

And more
There's also a large choice of
self-catering, B&B and hotel
accommodation in and around
Little Venice and Camden.
www.visitlondon.com

The Puppet Barge
Established in 1982,
the Puppet Theatre is
a floating theatre boat
moored in Little Venice
for most of the year. The
boat, which seats up to
55, also takes a theatre
tour of the Thames during
the summer.
T:0207 2496876
www.puppetbarge.com

How to get there

Train info

Paddington, Warwick Avenue & Camden Road
London Underground www.tfl.gov.uk
National Rail Enquiries T:08457 484950

Bus info

London Buses www.tfl.gov.uk

Parking

Car park at Paddington (charge)

Local Tourist info

London Tourist Information

T:08701 566366 www.visitlondon.com

London Canal Museum

Battlebridge Basin. Canalside museum in a
former ice warehouse. Displays on London's
canals, boats, cargo, people and horses -
including a huge ice well. Open Tues-Sun (&
Bank Hols) 1000-1630 (late opening last Thurs
in month). Small admission charge.
T:0207 7130836 www.canalmuseum.org.uk

London Zoo

The world's oldest scientific zoo, it has an
emphasis on education and conservation.
T:0207 7223333 www.zsl.org

Boats

Jason's Trip

Trip boat. Runs from Little Venice to Camden.
45 minutes one way, with commentary.
T:0207 2863428 www.jasons.co.uk

London Waterbus Company

Regular trips between Little Venice & Camden.
Can even drop off and pick up at the canal
entrance to London Zoo.
T:0207 4822550 www.londonwaterbus.com

Jenny Wren Canal Boat Cruises

Walker's Quay. Buffets & picnic baskets
T:0207 4854433 www.walkersquay.com

'My Fair Lady' Cruising Restaurant

Walker's Quay. Dinner and Sun lunch cruises.
T:0207 4854433 www.walkersquay.com

Avon gorge and aqueducts
Kennet & Avon Canal - Bath to Bradford on Avon

It's a city sculpted from pale-coloured local stone that has comfortably grown up with fashionable life; and to prove its credentials, today's Bath echoes with the decadence of bathing Romans and swaying crescents of Georgian airs and graces. But away from the woozy culture of spa water, a less hailed and quietly modest waterway swoops the urban edges of Bath.

The Kennet & Avon Canal opened in 1810 creating a revolutionary transport link from London to Bristol. Graceful Georgian ladies of Bath in their exquisite drapery may well have huffed at the arrival of the navvies, boatmen and canals; and even Jane Austen, one of Bath's most famous residents, might have mingled her own opinions amongst Regency gossip on such matters.

But from the start, the Kennet & Avon Canal made no apology and its bold locks still link the man-made canal to the River Avon on the south side of the city. The original canal architecture was firmly steered by influential local residents, giving this canal its unusual delicate ironwork bridges and others adorned with ostentatious stonework. Grand upright Georgian houses overlook the water as if still expressing their opinion. Even today, a generous percentage of occupants perpetuate Bath's reputation for affluence by cushioning their gardens with more expensive garden benches than most canalside gardens in other regions could muster. As views of the Abbey, Pulteney Bridge and Crescent Gardens get left behind, the canal reaches less populated climes. The fringes of the city might briefly splurge with graffiti, but the charms of the Kennet & Avon are soon allowed to come out and play with all your senses and sensibilities.

The canal saunters into golden Avon fields, so now you can slow your pace to really enjoy this walk. But try not to be enraged if you have to share the towpath with others: Bath to Bradford on Avon is part of the popular National Cycle Network and is well used all year round by cyclists wearing Bristolian hats and pannier-families saddled up for a grand day out. Intrepid walkers might even be disappointed by the over-cosseted hard-surfaced towpath on the Kennet & Avon since it's never rough rambling along the string thin, overgrown, clumpy towpath trail that some canals promise - but it's easy walking, and cool for ramblers who use wheelchairs, or family walkers who want to keep the kids interested by taking bikes.

This section of the Kennet & Avon gives you more than just a leafy walk, it's also a peep show at long lines of moored narrowboats. Live-aboards are attracted to this canal and winter brings a stem to stern community, sprawling with traditional narrowboat colours and hippy shades of pink, purple and sometimes shabby rust. The walk is dominated by a flotilla of eccentric living. Some boats are expensively bought, others are budget or shoestring, and some are blatantly homemade and could be confused with stage props for a Robinson Crusoe production - but all are fascinating to the passerby and home to someone.

This is a towpath walk blending cream-stone charisma with leafy Avon waters. It's close enough to town for the possibility of hearing duos of joggers panting office politics, and far enough away from town to meet leisurely walkers. Narrowboats laze around, oblivious to anything but the peace and quiet of their world.

CROSS GUNS

Claverton
Pumping
Station

TO START

Highlight of the walk

Dundas Aqueduct is a monumental work of classical art built in 1804 by John Rennie's architecture and engineering. Scramble down from the canal for a zoomed-out view from afar, then zoom in to look intimately at the stonework for the stonemasons' carved signatures. Avoncliff Aqueduct, further along, is similar in design but has been lovingly restored after dodgy times of neglect and unsympathetic ownership. If you can blink out the addition of safety railings, it's still an architectural gem carrying the canal over the river and the railway.

Did you know?

This entire walk follows Route 4 of Sustrans' National Cycle Network.

Fascinating fact

When cars arrived, the intrusion of road routes meddled with locks 8 and 9 and they were merged into one lock - over 19 feet deep (challenging the title of Tuel Lock on the Rochdale Canal as deepest lock on the waterways). If you like fairground thrills, peer down into the chasm, but hold onto your dogs, grab your children's hands, and stand back from the lock's side.

Start:
Bath
OS Grid ref: ST754643
Finish:
Bradford on Avon
OS Grid ref: ST825602
Distance:
9 miles approx
Terrain:
Easy walking
OS Explorer Map
- 155/156

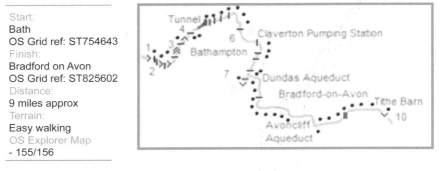

The walk - step by step

1. Where the canal joins the Avon just below Bath Bottom Lock (no.7), follow the towpath alongside the locks.

2. Locks 8 & 9 were merged making Bath Deep Lock one of the deepest (over 19ft) on the canal network.

3. Bath's trademark Georgian houses line the canal, and there are views over the city from the top lock.

4. At bridge 188 the towpath crosses sides by Bath Narrowboats base at Sydney Wharf, and again over Cleveland House Tunnel, before leaving the city past a long line of moored boats by views over the valley.

5. Any sound from the A4 disappears as the canal enters Bathampton, past the George and popular moorings, before veering off south to Claverton.

6. The canal is tree-lined with glimpses of fields before reaching Claverton Pumping Station, worth a diversion down over the railway. It used to pump water up from the Avon to the canal and, restored by the volunteers, it still works on special 'Pumping Days' (www.claverton.org).

7. About a mile further on, the towpath crosses sides again as you approach Dundas Aqueduct. A footbridge takes you over the entrance to Brassknocker Basin (the old Somersetshire Coal Canal) before you cross the aqueduct.

8. Beyond the aqueduct, trees close in again for the next couple of miles until open views around Avoncliff Aqueduct. Cross the aqueduct, and follow the towpath round to the left past the pub and tea room.

9. The canal follows the Avon for the next mile into Bradford on Avon. The canalside medieval Tithe Barn is surrounded by artists' studios, galleries, shops and a tearoom. (www.tithebarnartscrafts.co.uk)

10. The walk ends by Bradford Lock and the busy wharf above the lock.

Where to eat

George Inn
Bathampton. Canalside near bridge 183.
T:01225 425079 www.thespiritgroup.com

Raft Café Boat
Moored at Bathampton. T:07733 336989

Angelfish Restaurant
In Brassknocker Basin. T:01225 723483

Wheelwrights Arms
Monkton Combe. Short walk to Dundas Wharf.
T:01225 722287 www.wheelwrightsarms.co.uk

Hop Pole Inn
Limpley Stoke. In hotel grounds a short walk
from Limpley Stoke Bridge. T:01225 723134

Fordside Tea Rooms
Limpley Stoke. T:01225 722115

Cross Guns
Canalside by Avoncliff Aqueduct.
T:01225 862335 www.crossguns.net

The Mad Hatter Café Tearoom
By Avoncliff Aqueduct. T:01225 868123

Coffee Boat
Moored in Bradford on Avon. T:07815 138912

Lock Inn Café
Bradford on Avon. Canalside near Bradford
Lock. T:01225 868068 www.thelockinn.co.uk

Canal Tavern
Bradford on Avon. Canalside. T:01225 867426

Granny Mo's Tea Room
Bradford on Avon. Canalside by Bradford
Lock. T:01225 867515 www.grannymos.co.uk

Wharf Cottage Shop & Tearoom
Canalside by Bradford Lock. T:01225 868683

Barge Inn
Bradford on Avon. Canalside near the lock.
T:01225 863403

Best picnic spot
On the grass at Bathampton.

Bath
Large choice of other pubs and cafés in Bath
and Bradford on Avon.

Where to stay

Canalside B&Bs
Tolley Cottage
Bath. Canalside.
T:01225 463365
www.tolleycottage.co.uk

Canalside cottages
Berkeley Coach House
Limpley Stoke. Short walk from
bridge 175.T:01225 723956

Cross Guns
Canalside by Avoncliff
Aqueduct. Studio flat above pub
T:01225 862335
www.crossguns.net

Lock View Cottage 4-star
Bradford on Avon. Overlooking
the canal. T:01225 865607
www.lockviewcottage.co.uk

Canalside hotels
Best Western Limpley Stoke
3-star. Short walk from canal.
T:01225 723333
www.latonahotels.co.uk

Canalside pubs & Inns
Cross Guns
Canalside by Avoncliff
Aqueduct. T:01225 862335
www.crossguns.net

Wheelwrights Arms 4-star
Monkton Combe. Short walk to
Dundas Wharf. T:01225 722287
www.wheelwrightsarms.co.uk

Barge Inn
Bradford on Avon. Canalside
near the lock. T:01225 863403

And more
Good choice of self-catering,
B&Bs and hotels in and around
Bath and Bradford on Avon.
www.visitbath.co.uk

How to get there

Train info
Bath Spa, Avoncliff, & Bradford on Avon
National Rail Enquiries T:08457 484950
Bus info
Traveline T:0871 2002233
Parking
Several car parks to choose from in Bath

Local Tourist info

Bath Tourist Information Centre
T:0844 8475256 www.visitbath.co.uk
Bradford on Avon Tourist Information Centre
T:01225 865797 www.bradfordonavon.co.uk
Kennet & Avon Canal Trust
The Trust, based in Devizes has worked
tirelessly for over 40 years. Initially formed to
bring about the restoration of the Kennet &
Avon, its main objectives now are to continue
to protect, enhance and promote the canal.
T:01380 721279 www.katrust.org.uk

Boats

Holiday boat hire
Anglo Welsh Waterway Holidays
T:0117 3041122 www.anglowelsh.co.uk
Bath Canal Boat Company
T:01225 312935 www.bathcanalboats.co.uk
Moonraker Canalboats
T:07973 876891 www.moonboats.co.uk
Sally Narrowboats. Also day boats
T:01225 864923 www.sallyboats.ltd.uk
Boat Trips
Brassknocker Basin and Bradford on Avon
T:01380 721279 www.katrust.org.uk
Bath Narrowboats. Also day boat hire.
T:01225 447276 www.bath-narrowboats.co.uk
Day boat, Canadian canoe & bike hire
Brassknocker Basin, nr Dundas Aqueduct
T:01225 722292 www.bathcanal.com
Lock Inn, Bradford on Avon
T:01225 868068 www.thelockinn.co.uk

Canal on the beach
Bude Canal - Summerleaze to Marhamchurch

Britain's inland waterways fool you when you follow a canal towpath that lets ocean winds mess your hair and beach sand scuff inside your sandals.

The Bude Canal is different from most: it asks you to walk with seagulls, step over lobster pots and love it for its waterscape dotted with rowing boats rather than narrowboats.

And finally it surprises you with incongruous mighty lock gates tumbling straight onto the golden sands of a Cornish beach. Cornish coasts are notoriously rough but despite the will of the weather for over two centuries, the gates operate perfectly today.

The Bude Canal was built to carry mainly sand, limestone, coal and farm manures and, by 1825, 35½ miles of canal ran from the barge canal near the beach to smaller tub boat canals further inland.

When the railways reached Bude in 1898, the waterways closed and most sections were sold back to the landowners. A lost waterway, unwanted and unused, eventually allowed nature to reclaim the cut, returning it to a haven for rare species of flora and fauna.

Canal enthusiasts made sure that the two miles from Bude to Helebridge remained open and, over recent years, the Bude Canal Regeneration Project has drummed a stalwart battle to revitalize the canal.

Despite some rumbles of contention from different viewpoints, the towpath has been laid with a hard easy-walking surface making it easily accessible for most.

The vision for the future of the Bude Canal has oars, paddles, boots and cream teas in mind and that, along with seaviews from the towpath, gives this canal its distinctive holiday atmosphere. The wide lower wharf area has a real seaside feel - rowing boats for hire, food and ice creams for sale.

Tourists have flocked to Bude's beaches ever since the railways connected the corridors of the South West to outsiders. Today big waves attract surfers and the hyper cool factor that comes with them, while the canal manages to keep its secret haven from the crowds, with history still whispering romantically all along the way.

A walk along the Bude Canal today is like stepping into the past while at the same time scuffing your boots on the future.

But after a day of healthy exercise, the only way to end a walk along this canal is to sit on the beach and watch the sun go down over the water... with a Cornish ice cream in your hand, of course.

Did you know?

Bude Canal's sea lock is one of only two in the UK opening directly out to the sea and it's a Scheduled Ancient Monument. It was built to allow sea vessels into the wharf for trading and still operates today.

The lock was set in a huge breakwater to protect and enhance the wharf area and has had to be refurbished or repaired many times, the most recent being in 2008 when a storm wrenched one of the gates off its hinges!

Fascinating fact

Bude was the first canal in the UK (second in the world) to use water-powered tub boats. The canal was also the first in the world to use tub boats with permanent iron wheels. The boats needed the wheels so that they could be pulled on rails up the canal's six inclined planes (the most on any one canal).

The boats were hauled up the inclined plane to the next level by chains driven by huge underground water wheels (all except one which used huge water buckets). At the top of the inclined plane, the boats were refloated to carry on their way.

Start
Summerleaze Beach
OS Grid ref: SS203064
Finish:
Marhamchurch
OS Grid ref: SS221036
Distance:
2 miles approx
Terrain:
Flat easy walking until
the inclined plane at
Marhamchurch
OS Explorer Map - 111

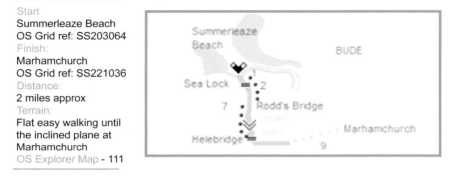

The walk - step by step

1. The huge sea lock marks the start of the Bude Canal.

2. Follow the towpath suspended over the beach for the first few yards.

3. Almost immediately you reach the wide lower wharf area.

4. Cross the road at the end of the wharf (Falcon Bridge is almost too low even for rowing boats to pass under!). The towpath continues from the car park by the Tourist Information Centre.

5. On the opposite side of the canal, you'll see evidence of older buildings such as the converted lifeboat house, now apartments, and a Grade II-listed building which was once a saw mill and later a steam laundry, before being converted into private homes in the 1980s (a couple are now available for holiday lets - see 'Where to stay' on the page opposite).

6. The towpath is fringed by trees to your left, hiding Bude Marshes, a nature reserve popular with twitchers, and the scenery opens out as fields dotted with sheep appear to the right.

7. At Rodd's Bridge, the towpath crosses over to the right side of the canal then continues along towards the canal's only other locks, Rodd's Bridge and Whalesborough, with open views of the Cornish countryside. The two locks have recently been restored, making this stretch navigable again.

8. Just before Helebridge, where the River Neet and the canal merge, you'll see a weir off to the left used to control the flow of water to the canal.

9. At Helebridge, continue under the A39 and walk the last few hundred tree-lined yards to the site of the canal's first inclined plane to Marhamchurch.

10. Continue up the hill to explore Marhamchurch (& catch the bus back to Bude) or turn around for a return walk along the canal.

Where to eat

Castle Restaurant & Tearoom
In the Castle Heritage Centre, at the wharf
Open daily 1000-1400 (Sundays to 1500) and
every evening except Sunday. T:01288 350543
www.thecastlerestaurantbude.co.uk

The Brasserie
Canalside at the wharf. Restaurant and café.
Ice creams too. T:01288 355275

Brendon Arms
Canalside by Falcon Bridge.
T:01288 354542 www.brendonarms.co.uk

Falcon Inn
(in Falcon Hotel) Canalside near Falcon
Bridge. T:01288 352005 www.falconhotel.com

Woodlands Tea Rooms
Helebridge. Short walk from the canal.
T:01288 361317

Bullers Arms Hotel
Marhamchurch. Short walk from the canal.
T:01288 361277 www.bullersarms.co.uk

Best picnic spot
By the sea lock overlooking the beach!

Bude
Large choice of other pubs and cafés in Bude.

Sir Goldsworthy Gurney 1793 - 1875
Known as Cornwall's 'forgotten genius',
the Victorian inventor devised a way to
build the castle (now Heritage Centre)
at Bude on sand - despite much initial
derision from his peers. Among his other
inventions were the first mechanised
steam-driven vehicle and limelight (used
in theatres, it lead to the use of the phrase
'in the limelight'). He also created the
'Bude' light, using limelight and an array
of lenses. It was used to light the Houses
of Parliament and applied to lighthouses,
saving countless lives.

Where to stay

Canalside cottages
Captain's Cottage, Bude.
Canalside near the sea lock
Lifeboat House Holiday
Apartments 3-star, Bude.
T:01288 354542
www.brendonarms.co.uk
Court Farm Holidays 4-star
Marhamchurch. Dog-friendly.
T:01288 361494/489
www.courtfarm-holidays.co.uk
Harbour Loft, Bude.
Overlooking beach & sea lock
T:01288 352082
www.harbourloft.co.uk
Mallards, The Old Laundry,
Bude. Canalside with private
jetty & rowing boat. Dog-friendly
T:01297 560033/560822
www.mallards-bude.co.uk
Primrose Cottage 4-star Bude.
Canalside near sea lock. Dog-
friendly. T:01288 354004
www.primrosecottagebude.co.uk
Seascape, Bude. Canalside
overlooking the beach
T:01288 356195
atlanticsaltaireholidays.co.uk
Stapletons, The Old Laundry
Bude. Canalside with private
jetty & boat T:07743 820293
www.theoldlaundrybude.co.uk

Canalside hotels
Falcon Hotel, Bude. Canalside
by Falcon Bridge T:01288
352005 www.falconhotel.com

Canalside pubs & inns
Brendon Arms 3-diamond
Bude. Canalside by Falcon
Bridge T:01288 354542
www.brendonarms.co.uk

And more
There's also a good choice of
self-catering, B&B and hotel
accommodation in and around
Bude. www.visitbude.info

Narrowboats and narrow locks

Worcester & Birmingham Canal - Alvechurch to Stoke Prior

Over 200 years ago, a line stretching thirty miles was furrowed out of the earth with shovels. At one end was Worcester and at the other Birmingham. A canal was born for the transportation of porcelain pots and the temptations of Cadbury's chocolate; and now, it lives on for holiday boats.

Despite the deception of a canal named after two cities, the towpath walker's treat lies in the rural miles between. But this isn't just a rural ramble - it's a journey that scrambles the Tardebigge, the longest lock flight in Britain: 30 locks with the audacity to carry narrowboats 220 feet uphill and downhill in still water. A staggering route with scenery dominated by black and white lock arms outstretched like chunky wooden wings in flight. Tardebigge isn't officially titled as one of the Seven Wonders of the Waterways, but stand still to digest the flight and you'll be convinced there should be an 'eighth'.

Despite being one of Britain's most lock-ridden waterways, the Worcester & Birmingham Canal is remarkably popular with holidaying boaters. In canal terms, a hilly journey is usually more of a physical workout for boaters than walkers; and the Tardebigge asks boat crews to brace themselves before their cog-winding journey that will take hours longer than the same amble would on foot. To make matters worse for the Tardebigge boater, no overnight mooring is allowed midway through the flight, so it's a gruelling, non-stop, 4-hour or more, ascent or descent (each narrow lock takes around 10 to 15 minutes to work through). The challenge makes the exhausted, the exhilarated and the simply fascinated share the flight with a tangible 'we're in it together' camaraderie.

On summer towpaths, walkers mingle with gongoozlers and everyone gets whisked into the boating experience; but in winter when there are fewer boats, the lone towpath walker is left with motionless water and hungrier views. Don't be put off by winter though; whether the flight is snow-covered or sun-scorched, you're treading in uplifting territory.

Climb the hillock overlooking the reservoir, about halfway through the flight, and views span as far as Worcestershire, Gloucestershire and Shropshire. This is Elgar's patch and his Malvern Hills peep from the distance, stringing music over the water.

And the water around these parts has inspired more than music. A plaque commemorates the famous meeting between Tom Rolt and Robert Aickman which took place aboard narrowboat Cressy, moored just above Tardebigge Top Lock. Rolt, Aickman and Narrowboat Cressy were the passion and brains behind the founding of the IWA (Inland Waterways Association) in 1946.

Their aim was to keep Britain's canal networks navigable yet it's not only boaters who are thankful for generations of volunteers such as the IWA who take up the battle to preserve this (and every other) waterway. It's fitting that such a mighty movement was born from a meeting on the brink of the equally bold Tardebigge Flight.

Highlight of the walk

The Tardebigge Flight is the longest
flight of locks in the UK, with 30
locks raising the canal 220 feet
in just over 2 miles. Tardebigge
Top Lock is one of the deepest
in Britain, with a rise of over 11
feet. Originally a boat lift was built
on the site but it was replaced by
an extra deep lock for technical
reasons and to save money for the
company building the canal.

Did you know?

The entire Worcester &
Birmingham Canal is part of the
Stourport Ring - one of the most
popular boating routes on the canal
network. The ring also includes
the Staffordshire & Worcestershire
Canal, the Birmingham Canal
Navigations (BCN) and the River
Severn. The canal is always busy
with boats being picked up and
dropped off at the home bases of
three major boat hire operators.

Look out for

The Birmingham, a tug built in
1912, is on display in the boat yard
at Tardebigge. The tug's primary
purpose was to pull working horse
boats through the canal's tunnels.

Start:
Alvechurch
OS Grid ref: SP022721
Finish:
Stoke Prior
OS Grid ref: SO951670
Distance:
6½ miles approx
Terrain:
Flat easy walking.
Can be muddy after rain.
OS Explorer Map
- 220/204

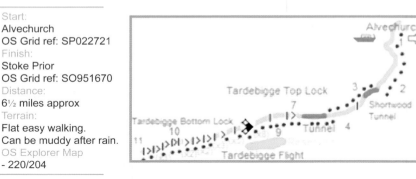

The walk - step by step

1. Turn left onto the towpath opposite the Weighbridge and Alvechurch boat yard, heading away from the village.

2. Just beyond bridge 59 and the pipe bridge, the surroundings become more wooded as you approach Shortwood Tunnel.

3. Follow the path uphill turning right over the tunnel. The path skirts the woods then heads across a field with open countryside views. Over a stile, you then rejoin the canal (on your left).

4. After about a mile, come off the canal by the base of Anglo Welsh hireboats, cross the bridge and turn right up the road. The canal is on your right but soon it disappears again into Tardebigge Tunnel.

5. At the top of the road, cross over and climb the stile into a field. Continue up the field, over another stile and down towards the A448. TAKE CARE as you cross the road.

6. Over another stile and uphill, the path then leads past a house to the road and, just opposite, rejoin the canal towpath.

7. Tardebigge Church is above you to the left and Tardebigge Wharf is on the opposite side of the canal.

8. Past Tardebigge Top Lock and lock cottage, there is a long stretch of moorings for visiting boats before the Tardebigge Flight begins in earnest.

9. The locks come in quick succession now past the reservoir on the left (climb up here for a view down towards the Malvern Hills).

10. Just beyond Tardebigge Bottom Lock and the line of moorings, go under the bridge by the Queen's Head opposite and immediately the first lock of the Stoke Flight is in view.

11. Opposite the Black Prince boat yard by Stoke Bottom Lock, turn right up the road for Stoke Prior village, the Navigation Inn and a bus back.

Where to eat

Crown Inn
Alvechurch. Canalside by bridge 61.
T:0121 4452300

The Weighbridge
Alvechurch. In Alvechurch Marina.
T:0121 4455111 www.the-weighbridge.co.uk

Swan Hotel
Alvechurch. In the village, a short walk from
the canal. T:0121 4455402

The Red Lion
Alvechurch. In the village, a short walk from
the canal. T:0121 4454162
www.vintageinn.co.uk/theredlionalvechurch/

Queen's Head Inn
Stoke Pound. Canalside by bridge 48 at the
bottom of the Tardebigge Flight.
T:01527 877777 www.queens-head-inn.co.uk

Navigation Inn
Stoke Prior. Short walk behind Stoke Wharf.
T:01527 870194

Boat & Railway
Stoke Works. Canalside by bridge 42.
T:01527 831065

Bowling Green
Stoke Works. Short walk from bridge 41.
T:01527 861291
www.freewebs.com/thebowlinggreen

Best picnic spot
Anywhere up the lock flight - plenty of
gongoozling opportunities as well as stunning
countryside around you.

Bromsgrove
Large choice of other pubs and cafés in
Bromsgrove.

Where to stay

Canalside B&Bs
Wharf Cottage
Stoke Prior. Canalside near
bridge 41. Log cabin, also
available for self catering.
T:01527 559339
wharfcottagebromsgrove.co.uk

Canalside cottages
Bottom Lock Cottage
Stoke Prior. Canalside by Stoke
Bottom Lock.
T:01527 577346

Lock Cottage
Tardebigge. Owned by the
Landmark Trust. Canalside by
lock 31.
T:01628 825925
www.landmarktrust.org.uk

Wharf Cottage
Stoke Prior. Canalside near
bridge 41. Log cabin, also
available for B&B.
T:01527 559339
wharfcottagebromsgrove.co.uk

Canalside hotels
Ladybird Hotel 3-star
Aston Fields. Approx 1 mile
south of bridge 51, near Aston
Fields station. Wheelchair
access. T:01527 889900
www.ladybirdlodge.co.uk

And more
There's also a good choice of
self-catering, B&B and hotel
accommodation in and around
Bromsgrove.
visitnorthworcestershire.com

How to get there

Train info
Alvechurch & Aston Fields (approx 1 mile from bridge 51)
National Rail Enquiries T:08457 484950
Bus info
Traveline T:0871 2002233
Parking
Roadside in the village or near the canal

Local Tourist info

Bromsgrove Tourist Information Centre
T:01527 831809

Worcester Birmingham Canal Society
Formed in 1969, the Society still plays an important role in conserving and improving the canal. They also hold monthly meetings, usually with a visiting speaker on varied waterways-related topics, which non-members are very welcome to attend.
www.wbcs.org.uk

Boats

Alvechurch Waterway Holidays
Alvechurch. Holiday boat hire. Main base of the largest narrowboat hire operator in the UK.
T:0330 3330 590 www.alvechurch.com

Anglo Welsh Waterway Holidays
Tardebigge. Holiday & day boat hire.
T:0117 3041122 www.anglowelsh.co.uk

Black Prince Narrowboat Holidays
Stoke Prior. Holiday boat hire.
T:01527 575115 www.black-prince.com

Red rock route

Staffordshire & Worcestershire Canal - Wolverley to Stourton

At first glance, the grey urban sprawl in the middle of any map of England might not attract a rambler's eye, but this towpath walk from Wolverley to Stourton can rival anywhere along the canals of Britain for sheer appeal. It's a leafy slice of tranquillity and a retreat from the treacherously nearby urban mess. The Staffs & Worcs Canal is a stunner.

Amongst boaters it's famous for its narrow winding route and roaring red sandstone rocks that perilously overhang the water. The canal is a boater's favourite for its distinctive beauty, and always popular, despite the menace of foxy rocks waiting to scratch the precious paintwork of narrowboats. The walker's secret amusement is to watch pale-faced helmsmen navigating with baited breath and scrunched eyes.

At the start of the walk, the tiny village centre of Wolverley is worth exploring before you head off down the towpath. There's a danger of the Lock Inn luring the weak-willed before their boots are even warmed up (if you're walkers like us, who are easily distracted by the thought of a cosy pub, it's probably a sensible idea to set off early in the morning before landlords are up). Forget your thirst and soak up the sweeping waterscape of the miles ahead, exploring this fascinating route that leads over the boundary from Worcestershire to Staffordshire. The towpath takes you past mysterious caves carved into the red sandstone, a historic toll house, wildlife and flora, canopies of trees and sheep-filled fields.

The full route of the Staffs & Worcs Canal runs just over 46 miles from the River Severn at Stourport, then climbing around the edge of the Black Country, up through Wolverhampton, and all the way to the junction at Great Haywood where it meets the Trent & Mersey Canal.

It was built to carry cargoes of coal, steel, carpets and all kinds of materials that scarcely fit the delicious green ambience of this waterway. When commercial traffic ceased, the canal would have been lost if not for the efforts of the Staffordshire & Worcestershire Canal Society. They saved a canal that has become one of the busiest and best in Britain for leisure boating (and gongoozling).

Stop for lunch at the Vine in Kinver, washed down by a pint of their delicious local real ale of course. Then drag yourself away because the Staffs & Worcs Canal has something special ahead. The whole walk is leafy and uplifting, but the highlight is the towpath from Hyde Lock to Stourton Junction.

Hyde Lock is one of the Britain's most idyllic canal locks, perched above the village of Kinver and looking down from a green woodland oasis. From here to Stourton, forget about the stresses of daily life, listen to the water. This is as good as walking gets.

Come in April to see the bluebells, come in summer when the trees are green, or come in autumn when they turn. Or just come in winter, the most peaceful season of all.

Highlight of the walk

Hyde Lock sits above the village of Kinver looking down from a woodland oasis, wafting a golden canopy in autumn and bleating with bluebells and lambs in spring.

Did you know?

Between bridges 26 and 27, a large stone was erected by the Staffs & Worcs Canal Society in 1999 to mark the border between Worcestershire and Staffordshire. The survival of the canal as a leisure destination is thanks to the tireless hard work of the Society.

Look out for

A small cave cut into the red sandstone at the side of Debdale Lock. This was formerly used as overnight stabling for the working boat horses.

Fascinating fact

The Staffordshire & Worcestershire Canal, opened in 1772, was one of the earliest canals built by the great canal engineer, James Brindley. This walk from Wolverley to Kinver dramatically highlights his preferred engineering method of following the contours of the land rather than using tunnels or locks.

Start:
Wolverley Lock
OS Grid ref: SO831791
Finish:
Stourton Junction
OS Grid ref: SO861848
Distance:
6½ miles approx
Terrain:
Flat easy walking. Can
be muddy after rain.
OS Explorer Map
- 218/219

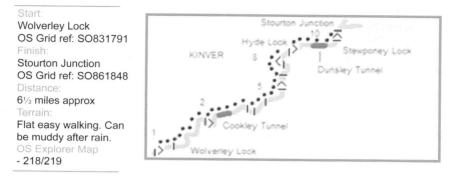

The walk - step by step

1. At Wolverley Lock, turn left onto the towpath with the canal on your right, and follow its winding leafy route through red sandstone and trees.

2. The canal bends almost back on itself then straightens up again towards Debdale Lock. An intriguing small cave at the lock was reputedly chiselled into the rock to provide overnight stabling for boat horses.

3. Once through the short Cookley Tunnel, look around and you'll see a row of cottages precariously perched above the tunnel.

4. A mass of red sandstone juts out so much here that it causes many a boat to scrape its paintwork while negotiating its way past.

5. The canal feels quite isolated for a while, passing a stone erected by the Staffs & Worcs Canal Society marking the border between Worcestershire and Staffordshire, before you arrive at Whittington Lock.

6. Houses speckle the route until the popular moorings below Kinver Lock remind you that this is a holiday location.

7. Walk through the tunnel below the lock then turn left onto the road to reach the Vine Inn.

8. Back on the canal, the towpath continues past Kinver's long residential moorings (there's a toilet and water tap halfway along them, but you will need a special BW key).

9. A treat awaits you after the moorings with one of the most idyllic locks to be found on Britain's canal networks, Hyde Lock. The canal turns the corner and, just after the short Dunsley Tunnel, you reach Stewponey Lock and its quirky toll house.

10. Just beyond the bridge is Stourton Junction, where the Staffs & Worcs Canal continues on and the Stourbridge Canal sets off to the right.

Where to eat

The Lock Inn
Wolverley. Canalside by Wolverley Lock.
T:01562 850581 www.thelockwolverley.co.uk

The Old Smithy Tearoom
Wolverley. Canalside by Wolverley Lock.
Run by the Lock Inn. Open 0900 to 1800 in
summer, 1000 to 1500 in winter.
T:01562 850581 www.thelockwolverley.co.uk

Bulls Head
Cookley. In the village. Garden overlooks the
canal. T:01562 850242

The Anchor Inn
Caunsall. A short walk from bridge 26.
T:01562 850254
www.theanchorinncaunsall.co.uk

Whittington Inn
Whittington. 300yds from bridge 28. Built in the
14th century by Dick Whittington's grandfather
T:01384 872110 www.whittingtonpub.co.uk

The Vine
Kinver. Canalside by Kinver Lock.
T:01384 877291

Kinver Brewery
Award-winning brewery set up in 2004,
producing beers named after the local
area such as 'Edge', 'Over the Edge' and
'Caveman'. www.kinverbrewery.co.uk

Enville Brewery
Brewing since 1993, Enville have a good
range of award-winning cask ales
www.envilleales.co.uk

Best picnic spot
Above Hyde Lock.

Kinver
Large choice of other pubs and cafés in Kinver

Where to stay

Canalside B&Bs
Southgate
Stourton. About a mile from
Stourton Junction.
T:01384 395229
southgatebedandbreakfast.co.uk

Canalside campsites
Camping & Caravanning Club
Site, Wolverley. Uphill from the
canal, just past the Lock Inn.
Open March to end October.
T:01562 850909
www.siteseeker.co.uk

Canalside hotels
Dunsley Hall Hotel
Kinver. Grade II-listed hotel
near Dunsley Tunnel.
T:01384 877077 or 877871
www.dunsleyhallhotel.co.uk

And more
There's also a good choice of
self-catering, B&B and hotel
accommodation in and around
Kidderminster & Kinver.
www.visitworcestershire.org
www.enjoystaffordshire.co.uk

North Worcestershire Path
This 27-mile waymarked
route runs from Kinver
Edge to the south of
Birmingham. The path
crosses the canal at
Caunsall Bridge, no.26,
and links with the
Worcestershire Way and
the Staffordshire Way at
Kinver Edge.

How to get there

Train info
Nearest train station is Kidderminster
National Rail Enquiries T:08457 484950
Bus info
Traveline T:0871 2002233
Parking
Lock Inn car park (if using pub) or roadside

Local Tourist info

Tourist info point: Kinver
(in 'Just Petals' shop) T:01384 877756

Kinver Edge
Owned and run by the National Trust.
Open all year.
T:01384 872418 www.nationaltrust.org.uk

Holy Austin Rock Houses
Owned and run by the National Trust. Cave
houses were dug into the soft red sandstone
of the area and lived in up to the 1950s. One
of the houses has been restored giving visitors
insight into Victorian life as a cave dweller.
Open March to 30 November Sat & Sun 1400-
1600 (Grounds open daily all year).
T:01384 872553 www.nationaltrust.org.uk

Staffordshire & Worcestershire Canal Society
Established in 1959, the Society's mission is
'to protect and promote the Staffordshire &
Worcestershire Canal (SWC) for the benefit
and enjoyment of all'.
T:01380 721279 www.swcs.org.uk

Boats

Anglo Welsh
Wootton Wawen.Holiday & day boat hire.
T:0117 3041122 www.anglowelsh.co.uk

Olde black and white England
Stratford-upon-Avon Canal - Lapworth to Stratford

Shakespeare's Stratford-upon-Avon is one of Britain's top tourist attractions but, luckily for walkers, few of the bard-seeking visitors who pilgrim here spot the canal quietly ambling past town. The poet himself knew not how romantic the canals be, since their arrival came too late for his pen.

This walk along the Stratford-upon-Avon Canal treads the heart of Shakespeare's own territory, beyond the River Avon, disappearing into the deepest greens of real Warwickshire countryside far from over-English shops choking on souvenired clichés. Genuinely quaint black and white cottages blend with canal structures painted in the traditional black and white colours of British Waterways; and green smells of earth are only mildly blighted by the occasional hum of the distant motorway.

Mary Arden's House is only a short diversion from the water at Wilmcote if you need a Shakespearian fix - but you will meet some unusual canal features along this walk that will vie for your undivided attention.

Mini aqueducts hang like chunky bathtubs over roads with cars passing underfoot. The aqueducts' towpaths are weirdly low, letting you stand with the water at waist height while you peer over the metal sides into the canal.

Then there are mysteriously shaped barrel-roofed lock keepers' cottages that line the water. The truth behind the quirk is purely practical: engineers building the Stratford Canal knew more about building bridges than houses, so when they had to build lock cottages for the lengthsmen, they adapted their skills, resulting in cottages with these curious barrel-shaped roofs (look out for the barrel-roofed garden shed erected on the canalside lawn of a local resident with a sense of humour).

Like most canals, the Stratford has at times faced struggles for its survival. In 1959 passionate protests riled against the canal's closure and gutsy restoration work from volunteers led to this section of the canal being reopened in 1964. Scattered along the canal, you'll spot the Stratford-upon-Avon Canal Society's (Sonacs) plaques commemorating its reopening.

Improvements to any of Britain's canals are usually welcome, but occasionally building and maintenance decisions can be controversial too. The Basin has recently been improved, including the removal of the David Hutchings Footbridge, built and installed by prisoners at Wormwood Scrubs and Birmingham. Many regret this loss.

Where the walk ends in Stratford town, you can admire the Royal Shakespeare Theatre on the waterside, with those lurking gangs of Montague geese and Capulet swans.

Then, after your day's peaceful walk it would almost be rude not to join tourists lolling on the grassy space on the banks of the River Avon and grab refreshments from the Baguette Barge or the floating ice cream van in the Basin!

SONACS

TO ALL THOSE WHO WORKED SO HARD TO SAFEGUARD THE SOUTHERN STRATFORD CANAL FOR FUTURE GENERATIONS, CULMINATING IN THE RE-OPENING ON 11ᵗʰ JULY 1964 BY HER MAJESTY QUEEN ELIZABETH THE QUEEN MOTHER.

"WE WERE NOT EXPERTS THEREFORE WE DID NOT KNOW WHAT COULD NOT BE DONE" DAVID HUTCHINGS M.B.E. PROJECT LEADER

WOOTTON WAWEN
AQUEDUCT

Highlight of the walk

The Stratford-upon-Avon Canal
has three unusual aqueducts – at
Yarningale, Wootton Wawen and
Edstone (also known as Bearley).
The towpath is level with the base
of the cast-iron canal trough and,
as you walk across, your eye is
level with boats which appear to
be sailing as if perched in a bath
tub. Each of the aqueducts has an
ornate display board.

Did you know?

The footbridges on the Stratford-
upon-Avon Canal were built in two
halves with a 1-inch gap to allow
ropes to pass through so that, in the
days of horse-towed narrowboats,
the boatman would not have to
untie his horse from the boat as he
walked along the towpath.

Fascinating fact

The National Trust appointed
David Hutchings to manage the
restoration of the southern section
of the Stratford Canal. From 1961
to 1964, volunteers from societies,
the Boy Scouts, the Army and even
prisoners from Winson Green in
Birmingham worked to restore the
canal. It was reopened to navigation
in 1964 by the Queen Mother.

Start:
Lapworth Locks
OS Grid ref: SP178714
Finish:
Stratford-upon-Avon
OS Grid ref: SP204548
Distance:
13 miles (10 to Wilmcote)
Terrain:
Flat easy walking. Can
be muddy after rain.
OS Explorer Map
- 220/205

The walk - step by step

1. The 26 locks of the Lapworth Flight spread nearly two miles, with the first & last four straggling away from the main flight.

2. Halfway down the flight, busy Kingswood Junction, with its moored boats, split bridges and white-washed cottages, connects the Stratford Canal to the Grand Union via a short boat-filled branch line.

3. The M40 crosses the canal just before Lapworth Bottom Lock though its noise can be heard for some time before and after. Peace soon returns as the canal continues its way through a landscape of fields, trees and sheep.

4. A traditional 'lengthsman's' cottage available for holiday lets is next to Lock 31, and the Fleur de Lys pub opposite provides a welcome break.

5. Past private moorings and the next two locks, is the first of Stratford Canal's unique aqueducts, Yarningale.

6. A mile further on, below Preston Bagot Bottom Lock, the surroundings turn ever more rural with just bridges, locks and the occasional house to distract your thoughts until you reach Wootton Wawen.

7. Just past the wide basin, home to Anglo Welsh Boats and the Navigation Inn, Wootton Wawen Aqueduct carries the canal over the main A34.

8. Back in rural landscape for nearly four miles, the only break is Bearley (or Edstone) Aqueduct, the longest of the three (and the longest in England), which carries the canal over a river, a road and the railway.

9. The canal then passes through the outskirts of Wilmcote before descending towards Stratford via the 11 Wilmcote Locks.

10. The towpath is wider and better-surfaced from Lock 40. The outskirts of Stratford are visible from Lock 44 onwards and the canal meets the river Avon in Bancroft Basin.

Where to eat

Boot Inn
Lapworth. Near Lock 14.
T:01564 782464 www.bootinnlapworth.co.uk

Navigation Inn
Lapworth. Canalside by bridge 65 on the Grand Union Canal. T:01564 783337 www.navigationinnlapworth.co.uk

Fleur de Lys
Lowsonford. Canalside near Lock 31.
T:01564 782431
www.fleurdelys-lowsonford.com

The Crabmill
Preston Bagot. Short walk from bridge 47A.
T:01926 843342 www.thecrabmill.co.uk

Navigation Inn
Wootton Wawen. Canalside by Wootton Wawen Aqueduct. T:01564 792676 www.the-navigationinn.co.uk

Mary Arden Inn
Wilmcote. Opposite Mary Arden's House, a short walk from bridge 59. T:01789 267030 www.mary-arden.co.uk

Masons Arms
Wilmcote. A short walk from bridge 59.
T:01789 297416

Pen & Parchment
Stratford-upon-Avon. Near Bancroft Basin.
T:01789 297697

Red Lion
Stratford-upon-Avon. Canalside near Bancroft Basin. T:01789 266858

The Encore
Stratford-upon-Avon. Opposite Bancroft Basin.
T:01789 269462 www.theencorestratford.co.uk

Baguette Barge & The Elizabeth (Avon Ices)
Stratford-upon-Avon. Moored in Bancroft Basin
T:07963 956720 www.thebaguettebarge.com

Best picnic spot
In Bancroft Basin, where canal meets Avon.

Stratford-upon-Avon
Large choice of pubs and cafés in Stratford.

Where to stay

Canalside B&Bs
The Old Post House
Wilmcote. A short walk from bridge 59. T:01789 292142 theoldposthousewilmcote.co.uk

Canalside cottages
Lengthsman's Cottage
Lowsonford. Owned by the Landmark Trust. Canalside by Lock 31. T:01628 825925 www.landmarktrust.org.uk

Acanthus Cottage & Apple Loft.
Wilmcote. Both 4-star. Short walk from bridge 59.
T:01789 205889
www.peartreecot.co.uk

1 Bancroft Place
Stratford-upon-Avon. Canalside studio. T:01295 690335

4 Bancroft Place 3-star
Stratford-upon-Avon. Canalside studio. T:01920 871849 www.4bancroftplace.com

20 Bancroft Place 4-star
Stratford-upon-Avon. Canalside apartment.
T:01789 266839
bancroftplaceinstratford.com

Canalside pubs & inns
Mary Arden Inn
Wilmcote. Opposite Mary Arden's House, a short walk from bridge 59. T:01789 267030 www.mary-arden.co.uk

And more
There's also a good choice of self-catering, B&B and hotel accommodation in and around Stratford-upon-Avon.
visitstratforduponavon.co.uk

How to get there

Train info
Lapworth (short distance from start of walk),
Wilmcote & Stratford-upon-Avon
National Rail Enquiries T:08457 484950

Bus info
Traveline T:0871 2002233

Parking
Roadside

Local Tourist info

Stratford-upon-Avon Tourist Information Centre
T:0870 1607930
www.shakespeare-country.co.uk

Stratford-upon-Avon Canal Society (Sonacs)
Formed in 1956, the society's objectives
include the use, maintenance and
improvement of all inland waterways,
especially the Stratford-upon-Avon Canal.
T:01564 783672
www.stratfordcanalsociety.org.uk

Royal Shakespeare Company (RSC)
Stratford-upon-Avon.
T:01789 403444 www.rsc.org.uk

Shakespeare Birthplace Trust
Stratford-upon-Avon. T:01789 296083
www.shakespeare.org.uk

Mary Arden's House
Wilmcote. T:01789 293455
www.shakespeare.org.uk

Boats

Anglo Welsh Waterways Holidays
Wootton Wawen. Holiday & day boat hire
T:0117 3041122 www.anglowelsh.co.uk

Countess of Evesham
Stratford-upon-Avon. Cruising restaurant boat.
Lunch & dinner daily all year. T:07836 769499
www.countessofevesham.co.uk

The lost waterway
Droitwich Canal - Hanbury to the Severn

No one in their right mind would want to spend a week on the M6 and call it a holiday. Two centuries ago, canals were designed to be the 4mph water-motorways of the Industrial Revolution, so when they were superceded by the railways and discarded by industry in the early 1900s, nobody saw any value in them as a place to go on a boating holiday. That's how so many of Britain's canals met their ugly fate. Abandoned, forgotten and doomed to dogged dereliction. Nobody cared about canals. The manmade waterways born for capitalism, died for the same cause.

The Droitwich Canal, like many others, despite its proud heritage, crumbled from neglect. Its purpose was mainly the transportation of salt. Droitwich and salt have a long-term relationship, and when the Romans settled here in about 47AD, they called the town Salinae, meaning salt, and Roman soldiers even received part of their pay (their salary) in salt.

The Domesday Book repeatedly mentions Droitwich and its natural asset of salt, and medieval Droitwich kept its meat fresh with local salt long before the discovery of electricity and the ludicrosity of monster floor-to-ceiling fridges existed. Later, when it was the leisure-seeking Victorians turn, they were bound to love their Spa town.

The arrival of canals helped the salt industry prosper in Droitwich and boats carrying salty cargoes kept the waterway busy until it officially closed in 1939. There was no turning back for the fortune of the canal and, if there had been a glimmer of hope, it would have been doused when the Second World War swamped Britain. The water-route was lost, unnavigable for boats and dryly overgrown for walkers. But it wasn't lost forever.

The energy and enthusiasm of entrepid leisure boaters in the early 1970s meant a new movement was growing. In 1973 the Droitwich Canal Trust formed and, after 65 years of neglect, the Droitwich Canal was loved again with a mighty £11million project to restore the waterway for boaters and towpath users.

Dredging, weeding, trenching, building, fundraising, WRG camps, duck races, boat trips; help came in every shape, with adrenalin, dedication and fun. Local councils, community groups, private individuals and businesses helped. The Waterways Trust, British Waterways, and the IWA worked ceaselessly. The Droitwich Canal whispered for help and the triumph of its restoration came from the cooperation and collaboration of many voices, but mostly its debt is to the solidarity, sweat and stalwart vision of 'mere' volunteers. We walkers owe our right to roam the towpath to those volunteers. Everyone knows waterways are built for boats, but all across Britain, canals are being maintained and restored, keeping a national network of towpaths open for ramblers, walkers and strollers too.

Where there were once dry armies of reeds, there is now water to follow. New red bricks cobble with the old and a lost route has come back to life. Quite rightly there's some champagne celebrating to be done over the reopening of this canal, but after all the singing and dancing, the walker can revel in the green solitude of an amazing water trail.

Thankfully, a canal once deemed worth its salt, is again.

waterway
recovery
group

Welcome to Vines Par

Please treat the

Highlight of the walk

Beyond the town, the views open out and the canal is at its rural best heading towards the River Severn. Untouched blankets of green are delicately scattered with ancient farm buildings that haven't been visually spoilt by corrugations of concrete extentions. If you allow your mind, it will hear a canal still whispering back to the 1770s.

Did you know?

Strictly speaking, the Droitwich Canal is two canals. The Barge Canal, engineered by James Brindley, was opened in 1771 to allow river barges (trows) to travel from the River Severn as far as Droitwich. The narrower Junction Canal was built later, in 1854, to connect Droitwich to the Worcester & Birmingham Canal at Hanbury.

Fascinating fact

Italian prisoners of war were put to work during the Second World War to fill in under one of the bridges in order to strengthen the road above (now the A449) for troop and tank movements. During the canal's restoration, a new tunnel was built next to this original one.

Start:
Hanbury Wharf
OS Grid ref: SO922629
Finish:
River Severn
OS Grid ref: SO842599
Distance:
7½ miles approx
Terrain:
Flat easy walking.
Can be muddy in rural
parts after rain.
OS Explorer Map - 204

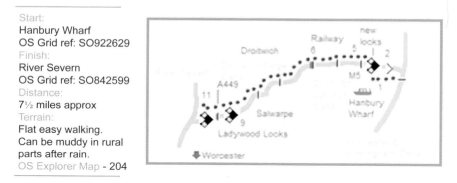

The walk - step by step

1. The walk starts at the junction of the Droitwich Canals with the Worcester & Birmingham, just across the road from Hanbury Wharf, a busy boatyard.

2. Just past the moored boats is the first of 3 Hanbury Locks, restored in 2002. When we first walked here in 2007, an army of reeds waited below the locks; now it's all clear as you follow the towpath to the first bridge.

3. Go up the steps, over the roadway, then rejoin the towpath down the steps on the righthand side of the canal, opposite newly created Gateway Park.

4. Follow the newly restored stretch of canal. Pass the brand new locks, then climb the steps by the next tunnel. Cross the road then go down the steps opposite.

5. The canal runs parallel to the road under the noisy M5, past another lock then reaches Vines Park, where the Junction Canal meets the Barge Canal

6. Continuing under the two railway bridges, the towpath runs alongside busy playing fields then, after another road bridge, leaves the town behind.

7. There are wide countryside views and a handy picnic bench by the remains of a former swing bridge.

8. The canal swings round under the bridge at the pretty village of Salwarpe (worth a detour to visit the church).

9. Back in open country, you reach the pretty lock house by the first of the four restored Ladywood Locks.

10. The black & white Porter's Mill sets the scene as you go under a couple of Grade II-listed red-brick bridges (typical of Brindley), before heading under the A449 and reaching the last two locks down to the River Severn.

11. A decision has to be made: head back to the A449 to catch a bus or taxi, or continue over fields by the river for three miles or so to Worcester.

Where to eat

Eagle & Sun
Hanbury. Canalside at Hanbury Wharf.
T:01905 770130 www.eagleandsun.com

Railway Inn
Droitwich. Canalside.
T:01905 770056

Gardeners Arms
Droitwich. Adjoining Vines Park by the canal.
T:01905 772936

Hadley Bowling Green Inn
Approx 1 mile north of Ladywood Lock. Has one of the oldest bowling greens in the UK and two AA rosettes for its food.
T:01905 620294
www.hadleybowlinggreen.com

Best picnic spot
There are a couple of picnic tables along the canal, best of which is around Salwarpe.
At the start of the Droitwich Canals at Hanbury Wharf, overlooking the junction itself, is a small picnic area. A plaque on an old lock arm dedicates the area to the memory of Brenda Morris, chairman of the Worcester Birmingham Canal Society.

Droitwich
Large choice of other pubs and cafés in Droitwich.

The shortest Ring
The restoration of the Droitwich Canal and its reopening brings to life a new cruising ring for boaters. It will be the shortest ring on the entire canal network. A 21-mile loop connecting the Droitwich with the River Severn and Worcester & Birmingham Canal.

Where to stay

Canalside B&Bs
Middleton Grange 4-star Silver Award. Salwarpe. Overlooking the canal. Dog-friendly.
T:01905 451678
www.middletongrange.com

Canalside campsites
Mill House Caravan & Camping Site, Hawford. Near the canal. Open April to October.
T:01905 451283

Canalside hotels
Raven Hotel
Droiitwich. In the town centre, a short walk from the canal.
T:01905 772224
www.raven-hotel.co.uk

Canalside pubs & inns
Hadley Bowling Green Inn 4-star. Approx 1 mile north of Ladywood Lock. The pub has one of the oldest bowling greens in the UK.
T:01905 620294
www.hadleybowlinggreen.com

And more
There's also a good choice of self-catering, B&B and hotel accommodation in and around Droitwich and Worcester.
www.visitworcestershire.org

...get outdoors and dirty

How to get there

Train info
Droitwich Spa
National Rail Enquiries T:08457 484950
Bus info
Traveline T:0871 2002233
Parking
Roadside

Local Tourist info

Droitwich Spa Tourist Information Centre
T:01905 774312 heritage@droitwichspa.gov.uk
Droitwich Canals Trust
Working with other members of the Droitwich
Canals Restoration Partnership to restore and
maintain the canals. (Reopen 2010)
T:01905 345307 www.worcs.com
Waterway Recovery Group
Established in 1970, the WRG works on
restoration projects all around the UK. They
run week-long working holiday camps and new
volunteers are always welcome.
www.wrg.org.uk
The Monarch's Way
This long-distance trail, 615 miles, follows the
route taken by Charles II during his escape
after the battle of Worcester in 1651. It joins
the Droitwich Canal for a short way before
heading off cross-country to the Stourbridge.
www.monarchsway.50megs.com

Boats

Drotiwich Canals Trust boat trips
Trips run every 1st and 3rd Sunday of the
month between April and October.
Wheelchair access. Booking essential.
T:07883 017818
Brook Line Narrowboat Holidays
Dunhampstead (on the nearby Worcester &
Birmingham Canal)
T:01905 773889 www.brookline.co.uk

Black Country glass trail
Stourbridge Canal - Delph Locks to Stourton

Stourbridge is no calendar town. Its canal, running through the heart of the industrial Midlands, might not boast the seductions of others such as the 'Mon and Brec' at the heart of a National Park, or the Rochdale gamboling gloriously towards the Pennines, but this Black Country trail will lead the walker straight to the soul of Britain's canals. Neither rural nor conventionally beautiful, but a walk not to miss.

Setting off from the metropolis of materialism, Merry Hill Shopping Centre, the canal ironically takes you quietly away from the consumer mayhem that it so successfully created in the 18th-century Industrial Revolution.

The towpath trails effortlessly from the shopping mall into an industrial landscape, then miraculously finds haven-pockets of green humming with wildlife and narrowboats. Urban canals are often described as linear parks, but this canal is always more than just that. History runs riot, playing with your imagination the whole way.

The area once thrived on industries around local coalmines and Stourbridge became world renowned for glass making. One of those glass cone furnaces has survived, and it stands like a cathedral of the glass industry on the landscape. The Red House Glass Cone is a surprisingly awesome sight that makes you feel as close to the beauty of canals as any of the leafier miles ahead.

The Black Country may not be renowned for royal blood, but you're walking in the footsteps of royalty. The Monarch's Way, a long-distance trail of 615 miles, follows the route taken by Charles II during his escape after the battle of Worcester in 1651. It joins the canal at Stourbridge, follows along the Town Arm and down to Stourton Junction before continuing right along the Staffs & Worcs Canal.

In parts, the canal visibly functions as an outdoor social club, buzzing with every generation from the local community. It's a tangible reminder of how canals serve as vital outdoor spaces in densely populated zones and the importance of waterways regeneration projects and the need for constant maintenance. It's always a continuous battle to keep canals open.

This canal has a reputation of defiance and its clear waters won't give away any secrets of its feisty past. But a small plaque mounted at Stourton Junction marks the 40th anniversary of the reopening of the Stourbridge Canal. It reminds us to pay tribute to the plucky people of the famous 1962 IWA (Inland Waterways Association) Rally, known as the battle of Stourbridge, who challenged the canal's closure and pressured the move to reopen it in 1967.

This is a fascinating walk with a friendly local feel, oozing with history, alive with Black Country culture and extraordinary charisma. The ugly duckling of walks, daring to adventure into unconventional walking territory, unforgettably beautiful.

RTO

Stourbridge Sixteen Locks

Locks 13 to 16 | Locks 1 to 12

← STOURBRIDGE CANAL TOWPATH →

Highlight of the walk

The Red House Glass Cone, 100ft tall, is one of only four surviving cones in Britain, and one of the most complete cone sites in Europe.

Don't resist having a look inside - it's now a museum and visitors can stand right where furnaces used to burn. From inside the cone, the sweat of the Industrial Revolution is tangible, especially if you look upwards from the centre through the bricked tunnel to the sky.

This is a place where you can let your imagination run wild. Cut glass and Art Deco-inspired pieces would have been unaffordable for glassmakers working insufferable bone-burning hours, and this place was probably more like Hell's flames to them than the breathtaking beauty it is today.

Have a cuppa in the museum's canalside café and sit outside to see where raw materials of coal and sand were once unloaded from narrowboats and cargoes of finished glass loaded back on.

Open all year daily 1000-1600 Admission free T:01384 812750 www.dudley.gov.uk

Start:
Delph Locks
OS Grid ref: SO918863
Finish:
Stourton Junction
OS Grid ref: SO861851
Distance:
5¼ miles (Town Arm 1¼)
Terrain:
Flat or downhill easy
walking.
OS Explorer Map - 219

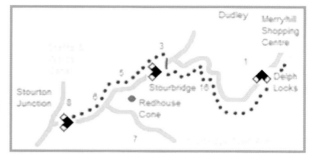

The walk - step by step

1. Turn left onto the towpath by Dudley No.1 Canal's Delph Locks.

2. The tree-lined canal, with odd glimpses of flats through the trees, turns more industrial up to Bowen's Bridge as small factories and moored boats line one side of the canal, before returning to leafy dominance.

3. The canal widens as it turns the corner to Leys Junction, where the Stourbridge carries on to the left while the short Fens Branch heads off right, to Fens Pool Nature Reserve.

4. Stourbridge Sixteen Locks start at Leys Junction. Cross the bridge to continue down the flight on the opposite side, past the entrance to Buckpool Nature Reserve and, after the next two locks, the Samson and Lion pub.

5. Past the next few locks, the dramatic scene with the Red House

Glass Cone in the distance opens out by the Dock stores and Dadford's Shed (named after the canal's engineer, Thomas Dadford) - a good place to linger and look at the old working boats before continuing past the Cone (to visit, go under the road bridge, then turn back up to the road).

6. Continuing past old warehouses (to be transformed into housing), you approach Wordsley Junction, where the canal continues straight ahead.

7. Well worth a diversion, the short Town Arm leads off left to Stourbridge. It is lined with warehouses & evidence of the glass industry including signs for Tudor Crystal & Ruskin Glass Centre, and ends by moorings at the Bonded Warehouse.

8. From Wordsley to Stourton Junction, the canal becomes rural again, and residential areas only reappear as you near the four locks leading down to the junction of the Stourbridge with the Staffs & Worcs.

Where to eat

Crystal Tearooms
Red House Glass Cone. Canalside.
Open daily 1000-1600
T:01384 812750 www.dudley.gov.uk

Moorings Tavern
Stourbridge. Canalside at end of Town Arm.
T:01384 374124

Samson & Lion
Wordsley. Canalside near lock 5. Over 200
years old, the pub used to be busy with
passing boat trade and provided stabling for
working boat horses. T:01384 77796

Tenth Lock
Brierley Hill. Canalside at foot of Delph Locks
T:01384 79041 www.tenthlockpub.co.uk

The Vine
Home of Bathams Brewery. Well worth the
short walk uphill from Delph Locks to this
authentic Black Country pub with real charm
and superior real ales – one of our favourites!
T:01384 78293 www.bathams.co.uk

Best picnic spot
Overlooking the locks by Dadford's Shed

Stourbridge
Large choice of pubs and cafés in Stourbridge.

International Festival of Glass

Once world-renowned for glassmaking
and now as a glass centre, Stourbridge
is proud of its heritage. The International
Festival of Glass, held every two years,
is a celebration of everything in glass:
workshops, events, exhibitions, glassmaking demonstrations, master classes
and more. www.ifg.org.uk

Where to stay

Canalside B&Bs
Southgate
Stourton. About a mile from
Stourton Junction.
T:01384 395229
southgatebedandbreakfast.co.uk

Canalside cottages
The Barn 4-star
New Wood Farm, Stourton.
Short walk from canal.
T:01384 390520
www.blackcountrystays.com

Canalside hotels
Copthorne Hotel 4-star
Merry Hill. Canalside on Dudley
Canal near Merry Hill Shopping
Centre.
T:01384 482882
www.millenniumhotels.co.uk

Canalside pubs & inns
Moorings Tavern
Stourbridge. Canalside at the
end of the Town Arm.
T:01384 374124

And more
There's also a good choice
of self-catering, B&B and
hotel accommodation in and
around Stourbridge or nearby
Kidderminster.
www.visittheheart.co.uk

How to get there

Train info
Stourbridge Junction & Stourbridge Town
National Rail Enquiries T:08457 484950
Bus info
Traveline T:0871 2002233
Parking
Car park at Merry Hill, short walk above Delph
Locks (charge)

Local Tourist info

Tourist info point: Kinver
(in 'Just Petals' shop) T:01384 877756
Buckpool & Fens Pools Nature Reserve
Stourbridge Canal T:01384 812780
Stoubridge Navigation Trust
The Trust aims to maintain the Stourbridge
Arm and the four historic buildings associated
with it. T:01384 395216
www.thebondedwarehousestourbridge.co.uk
The Bonded Warehouse
Stourbridge. Grade II-listed building restored
by the Stoubridge Navigation Trust. Used for
events and private functions.
T:01384 395216
www.thebondedwarehousestourbridge.co.uk
The Monarch's Way
More information on this long-distance trail
www.monarchsway.50megs.com

Boats

Blackcountry Man
Stourbridge. 3-hour cruise from the Bonded
Warehouse April-Oct Sundays at 1430. Also
special trips & charters. Wheelchair access.
Blackcountry Man Canal Shop sells gifts,
guidebooks and canalia.
T:01384 375912
www.canalboattripsstourbridge.co.uk

PEAK FOREST CANAL SOCIETY

This plaque was erected to
celebrate the efforts of the
Peak Forest Canal Society
and all other volunteers who
worked to recreate the
Cheshire Ring

IWA — The Inland Waterways Association

Commissioned by Manchester Branch

Silk and snakes
Macclesfield Canal - Macclesfield to Marple

Relics of the textile industry, Hovis bread and an unspoilt green landscape wash together in the peaceful waters of the Macclesfield Canal. Former mills now turned into offices still manage to muster thoughts of flour and silk as you follow the towpath deep into countryside leading to The North.

It's not as insalubrious as it might seem to start in the town of Macclesfield, with a short trot from the train station taking you along stereotypically cobbled patches signposted with names like 'Coronation Street'. As you reach the canal, you'll pass the original Hovis Mill where it's hard not to slip into Dvorak and sepia images of a knobbly-kneed boy on his bike delivering bread.

A few strides along the towpath and around the first bend, your world turns green with views over the Peak District forcing you to enjoy this lazy waterside walk.

Only a random nicotine whiff from the office break over the hedgerow reminds you of the conurbation being left behind, and the further north you venture, the more peaceful this walk becomes.

The towpath feels isolated in parts and allowed to be tufty underfoot (rather than ruined by hard surfacing as some other towpaths have been).

The Macclesfield Canal never sews sequins onto its frock, nor can-cans to get an audience, so when you stumble on its treasures, the rewards are intimately felt. Heritage is rife, and beautifully understated.

Keep your eyes peeled for the magnificent milestones along the way. They are unusually large for canal milestones, and made from Kerridge stone. The stones may appear humble, yet typically manage to seclude bigger canal secrets: once they would have kept tags on miles travelled by working boat crews, but during the Second World War, the stones were buried to stop potential enemy invaders from finding their way around. After the war, many were lost until canal enthusiasts in the 1980s found and restored the majority of them to their modest glory.

The Macclesfield is most renowned for its unique snake bridges, so watch out for them along the way. They swirl with perfectly spiralled brickwork once enabling boat horses to swap sides on the towpath without needing to be uncoupled from their narrowboats.

Marple Junction is where the Macclesfield and Peak Forest Canals meet, surrounded by views towards the Goyt Valley and wistful mountain peaks. It is worth the extra stroll to follow the Peak Forest Canal left as it heads northwards away from the junction and downhill through the dramatic flight of 16 locks (see page 183).

From the junction, if you have time to carry on, follow the Peak Forest Canal southwards and only stop walking when you really have to.

Highlight of the walk

Known by locals as the Happy Valley, Bollington feels more like a village than a town. Bollington Discovery Centre is in the canalside Clarence Mill. A gallery, displays and an image database tell the story of the town, the mill (and other cotton mills in the area), the Macclesfield Canal and their historic importance to the town. Regular exhibitions of art and local history. Canalside Community Radio is also based in the mill.

Open Weds 1330-1600 (Sat/Sun 1100-1600) T:01625 572985 www.happy-valley.org.uk www.ccr-fm.co.uk

Fascinating fact

The National Trust's Lyme Park, a short walk from bridge 17, featured as Darcy's house 'Pemberley' in the BBC's 1995 adaptation of 'Pride & Prejudice'.

T:01663 762023 www.nationaltrust.org.uk

Did you know?

The Macclesfield Canal is part of the Cheshire Ring, both a popular boating route and towpath walk. The Ring, 97 miles, covers all of the Macclesfield Canal and parts of the Rochdale, Bridgewater, Peak Forest, Ashton and Trent & Mersey Canals.

Start:
Bridge 38, Macclesfield
OS Grid ref: SJ925731
Finish:
Marple Junction
OS Grid ref: SJ961884
Distance:
11 miles approx
Terrain:
Flat easy walking. Muddy
in rural parts after rain.
OS Explorer Map
- 268/277

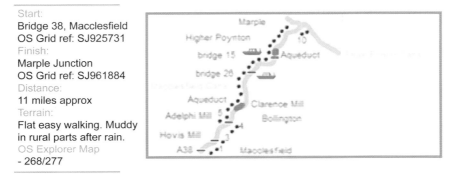

The walk - step by step

1. Start the walk at bridge 38, just by the boatyard.

2. Turn right onto the canal and follow the towpath past the imposing Hovis Mill opposite, the original flour mill now converted into plush apartments.

3. The town is mostly below the canal to the left and, by the time you reach bridge 36, stunning open countryside views are opening up around you. Houses line the canal for a short patch again, then it's open fields, hills and trees all the way to Bollington.

4. The towpath crosses sides at Clarke Lane Bridge (no.29), one of the Macclesfield's famous 'snake' bridges, curling round across the canal.

5. As you reach Bollington, another mill is on your left opposite the boatyard with its tantalising canalside café. Adelphi Mill used to produce silk but has now been converted into smart contemporary offices.

6. The canal passes Bollington on an embankment overlooking the town.

7. Just past a short aqueduct, you reach the huge Clarence Mill on the other side of the canal. A footbridge (bridge 26A) over the canal by the mill was completed in 2009 enabling walkers to visit the Discovery Centre and canalside café.

8. Just beyond bridge 26, open countryside surrounds the canal again and, apart from a short wooded area, remains all the way to Higher Poynton.

9. There's a tearoom and restaurant opposite a marina full of moored boats just past bridge 18. The canal widens by Higher Poynton's boatyard and chandlery after bridge 15.

10. Apart from a brief interlude in the small town of High Lanes, it's open countryside all the way to Goyt Mill on the outskirts of Marple. The towpath crosses sides at bridge 2 before Marple Junction, where the Macclesfield meets the Peak Forest.

Where to eat

Puss in Boots
Macclesfield. By bridge 37. T:01625 423261

Dani's Café & Wine Bar
Bollington. Canalside at Bollington Wharf opposite Adelphi Mill. Open daily 0900-1700. T:01625 573100 www.white-nancy.co.uk

Waterside Café
Clarence Mill, Bollington. Canalside (cross the new footbridge 27A). Open Mon-Fri 0930-1630, Sat/Sun 1000-1630. T:01625 575563

Vale Inn (and micro brewery)
Bollington. Short walk from bridge 26. T:01625 575147 www.valeinn.co.uk

Bollington Brewing Co T:01625 575380 www.bollingtonbrewing.co.uk

Windmill Inn
Whitley Green. Short walk from bridge 25. T:01625 574222 www.thewindmill.info

Miners Arms
Adlington. Near bridge 18. T:01625 872731

Lyme Breeze Restaurant & Tearoom
Adlington. Canalside. T:01625 871120

Boar's Head
Higher Poynton. Short walk from the canal. T:01625 876676

Coffee Tavern
Higher Poynton. Next to the Boar's Head.

The Trading Post
Higher Poynton. Canalside by bridge 15. T:01625 872277 www.canaltradingpost.co.uk

Bulls Head
High Lane. Canalside. T:01663 762070

Ring O' Bells
Marple. Canalside by bridge 2. T:0161 4272300 www.ringobellsmarple.co.uk

Best picnic spot
Between bridges 29 and 30.

And more
Choice of other pubs & cafés in Macclesfield, Bollington and Marple.

Where to stay

Canalside B&Bs
Red Oaks Farm 4-star
Bollington. A short walk from bridge 28 (the canal runs along their fields). T:01625 574280 www.redoaksfarm.co.uk

Canalside campsites
Jarman Farm Caravan Site Sutton Lane Ends. Short walk from Gurnett Aqueduct. Camping & Caravanning Club members only. T:01260 252501 www.jarmanfarm.com

Elm Beds Caravan & Camping Site, Higher Poynton. Canalside between bridges 15 & 16. T:01625 872370 www.peaksandplains.co.uk

Canalside cottages
East Lodge, Lyme Park Disley. In the grounds of Lyme Park, short walk from bridge 17. T:0844 8002070 www.nationaltrustcottages.co.uk

Canalside hotels
Best Western Hollin Hall Hotel, Bollington. A short walk from bridge 28. T:01625 573246 www.hollinhallhotel.com

Canalside pubs & inns
Church House Inn 3-star Bollington. In the village, a short walk from Bollington Aqueduct. T:01625 574014 thechurchhouseinn-bollington.co.uk

And more
Good choice of self-catering, B&Bs and hotels in and around Macclesfield and Bollington. www.visitcheshire.com

How to get there

Train info
Macclesfield, Poynton, Middlewood & Marple
National Rail Enquiries T:08457 484950
Bus info
Traveline T:0871 2002233
Parking
Roadside

Local Tourist info

Macclesfield Tourist Information Centre
T:01625 504114
Email: macclesfieldtic@cheshireeast.gov.uk
Macclesfield Canal Society
Formed in 1984, their primary aim is to
promote the canal for the benefit of all users.
www.macclesfieldcanal.org.uk
Macclesfield Silk Museums
At the height of the Silk Industry, there were
120 mills and dye houses in Macclesfield and
silk is still being produced there, albeit on a
much smaller scale. The history of the silk
industry and Macclesfield's role in it is now
best understood by visiting one of the four Silk
Museums, with exhibits ranging from restored
Jacquard handlooms and a huge collection
of silk ties to a photo archive containing over
20,000 photographs relating to Macclesfield
and the silk industry. Opening times vary.
T:01625 612045
www.macclesfield.silk.museum

Boats

Freedom Boats
Macclesfield. Day boat hire and trip boat.
T:01625 420042 www.freedomboats.co.uk
Braidbar Boats
Higher Poynton. Boatbuilder. Holiday boat hire.
T:01625 873471 www.braidbarboats.co.uk
Trading Post
Higher Poynton. Day boat hire.
T:01625 872277 www.canaltradingpost.co.uk

Land of mills and moors
Huddersfield Narrow Canal - Diggle to Slaithwaite

Wooden signposts splitting from weather, mosses, lichens and dry stone walls. With hardy grasses under your boots, you know you're treading proper walking ground, and this canal towpath proves it as it crosses one of the greatest and most gruelling of the National Trails, the Pennine Way.

The surroundings are a 'Last of the Summer Wine' film set, with Nora Batty battleaxing in one direction while the silence of the moors call in the other. The canal walks through the textile industry of the Industrial Revolution, but clogs have been replaced by walking shoes these days and the air is as clean as a whistle.

This section of the Huddersfield Narrow Canal was built in 1798 but the canal engineers had to overcome some construction difficulties before the first boat was able to travel through Standedge Tunnel almost 12 years later. The tunnel took 17 years to build and was finally opened in 1811. It is 5,029m long, 196m above sea level, 194m below the moors – making it the longest, deepest, highest canal tunnel in Britain, and officially one of the Seven Wonders of the Waterways.

Modern gates have been fitted above the tunnel entrance, sculpted with ironwork figures legging a narrowboat into the tunnel. Spare some pity for the characters they represent and their miserable journey, then take the high walk above the top of the canal on the moors. Unusually for a canal walk, the moors expect you to take care and orienteer the path.

The fate of the canal left it abandoned in 1944. The canal, the tunnel and the life-stories of navvies and working boatmen were cast aside for the railways. The Huddersfield Narrow Canal has only recently been reopened after years of dereliction. Thanks to the efforts of the Huddersfield Canal Society, in 1998 the guillotine tail gate at Lock 24E was restored to become the only working example remaining on Britain's canals, and the entire canal reopened to navigation in 2001.

This part of Yorkshire has feisty roots with courageous canal heritage, a determined mill industry and other episodes such as the fury of Marsden Luddites and local suffragettes.

But it has always known how to party too, and these days outsiders turn up in droves to join in. Slaithwaite (pronounced 'Slawit') has become so famous for its Moonraking Festival in February that the festival has now been changed to every other year, as the village was bursting at the seams with processions of lanterns and folkie legends. The canal trails straight through the town as if the water was the main street itself, giving Slaithwaite genuine, non-fussy, canal character.

The Huddersfield Narrow is a canal worth celebrating, not just because it was once a shockingly defiant canal that simply didn't care if the Pennines got in the way, but also because the triumph of its restoration happens to be an exciting walk. Sheepdogs and mills mingle on the moorlands and, all the way, the canal tells the story of both.

Highlight of the walk

Standedge Tunnel & Visitor Centre. Take a boat trip into the longest, deepest, highest tunnel in the UK.

www.standedge.co.uk

Did you know?

Mikron Theatre, the travelling theatre company, are based in Marsden. They spend the summer touring the canal networks by narrowboat, and do a road tour off season. A registered charity, they're always grateful for support! Why not join the 'Friends of Mikron'?

www.mikron.org.uk

Fascinating fact

Marsden has a reputation for festivals. One of its most popular is Moonraking. The story goes that in 1802 two Slaithwaite rogues were smuggling liquor in barrels on the canal when disturbed by patrolling soldiers. The rogues hid the barrels in reeds, and returned that night to collect them. Caught again, the quick-witted rogues yelled, "Cans tha noon seah? T'mooin fell int watter an we'ar rekkin er aht!" The soldiers went off sniggering at their stupidity. Today the smugglers' triumph is a good excuse for a carnival - lanterns floating down the canal, music and a giant Mr Moon.

www.slaithwaitemoonraking.org

Start:
Diggle
OS Grid ref: SE006079
Finish:
Slaithwaite
OS Grid ref: SE079139
Distance:
7 miles approx
Terrain:
Flat easy walking on towpath. More difficult terrain on moor over tunnel. Boggy after rain.
OS Explorer Map - OL1/OL21/288

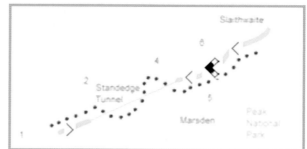

The walk - step by step

1. From the tunnel mouth at Diggle, follow the signs for the Standedge Trail up over the tunnel onto the moor.

2. TAKE CARE when walking the trail over the moorland. The weather can change very quickly, and it's sensible to go prepared with waterproofs and an OS map or Standedge Trail leaflet.

3. The views over the surrounding countryside and valley are stunning. You can follow the trail either to the left (close to the route of the road) or to the right (directly across the moor).

4. Whichever route you choose, you'll cross over the Pennine Way. When you arrive at Tunnel End, come down to explore Standedge Tunnel's entrance, the Visitor Centre and café.

5. Leaving the tunnel behind, follow the towpath under the bridges towards Marsden. It's worth a detour into the village, and the National Trust office's exhibition. Marsden is steeped in the history of weaving and has often been used for filming 'Last of the Summer Wine' and 'Where the Heart is'.

6. Back on the wide towpath, you'll pass the series of 18 locks taking the canal down towards Slaithwaite.

7. The canal is mostly tree-lined but views ahead show hills and moorland and there are frequent reminders of weaving industry and mill heritage. Just beyond Sparth Reservoir, the views open up for a while before becoming more enclosed again as you pass Lingards Wood and Milnbridge.

8. As you approach Slaithwaite, the canal seamlessly brings the country into the town. It's the only town in the UK with a canal along its main street.

9. Past the guillotine lock and a former mill housing the Empire Brewery, just above lock 23E, there's a welcome sight of tables on the canalside next to the permanently moored floating café. The huge Globe Worsted Mill, sadly now closed, dominates the centre.

Where to eat

The Diggle Hotel
Diggle. Near the tunnel portal.
T:01457 872741 www.saddleworthlife.com

Tunnel End Inn
Marsden. A short walk from the canal, overlooking the tunnel entrance.
T:01484 844636 www.tunnelendinn.com

Standedge Tunnel Water's Edge Café
Marsden. Canalside by tunnel entrance. Open daily 1000-1700 Apr-Aug 1000-1600 Sept-Oct. (Closed Mon - not Bank Hols & summer)
T:01484 844298 www.standedge.co.uk

Riverhead Brewery Tap & Dining Room
Marsden. In the village, a short walk from the canal. Micro-brewery on site.
T:01484 841270 www.ossett-brewery.co.uk

Moonraker Floating Tearoom
Slaithwaite. Narrowboat café moored by Dartmouth Lock (23E). Open Tues-Sun all year (winter openings vary). T:01484 846370

The Little Bridge
Slaithwaite. Café wine bar, canalside by bridge 44. Open Wed-Sun.
T:01484 846738

The Wharfeside Inn
Slaithwaite. Short walk from canal.
T:01484 847333

Empire Brewery
Slaithwaite. Only brewing since 2004, Empire have a range of cask ales including 'Strikes Back' (easily recognisable to Star Wars fans!)
T:01484 847343

Best picnic spot
On the moor overlooking Standedge.

And more
Large choice of other pubs & cafés in Marsden and Slaithwaite.

Where to stay

Canalside B&Bs
Sunfield Accommodation 2-star Diglea, Diggle. A short walk from the tunnel mouth.
T:01457 874030
www.sunfieldaccom.co.uk

Canalside cottages
Crow Hill Cottages 5-star Marsden. On the edge of Marsden Moor, a short walk from the canal. T:07836 778728
www.crowhillcottages.co.uk

Canalside hotels
Hey Green Country House Hotel 2-star, Marsden. On the edge of the moor, a short walk from Standedge Tunnel entrance and Visitor Centre.
T:01484 848000
www.heygreen.com

Canalside pubs & inns
Tunnel End Inn
Marsden. A short walk from the canal, overlooking the tunnel entrance. Self-contained apartment. T:01484 844636
www.tunnelendinn.com

Olive Branch Restaurant with Rooms 4-star
Marsden. Short walk from canal. T:01484 844487
www.olivebranch.uk.com

And more
There's also a good choice of self-catering, B&B and hotel accommodation in and around Marsden and Slaithwaite.
www.yorkshire.com

How to get there

Train info
Marsden, Slaithwaite & Greenfield (2 miles from Diggle at start of walk)
National Rail Enquiries T:08457 484950
Bus info
Traveline T:0871 2002233
Parking
Car parks at Standedge/Marsden or roadside

Local Tourist info

Marsden Information Point
T:01484 845595 www.kirklees.gov.uk
Huddersfield Narrow Canal Society
Originally set up in 1974, the Society initially campaigned vigorously (and successfully) for the complete restoration of the canal. They can now concentrate on its maintenance and promotion e.g. photographic 'Towpath Guide'.
T:01457 871800 www.huddersfieldcanal.com
'Welcome to Marsden' Exhibition
In the National Trust Estate Office by Marsden railway station. Displays, leaflets and info about Marsden and Upper Colne Valley.
Open daily 0900-1700.
T: 01484 847016 www.nationaltrust.org.uk

Boats

Standedge Tunnel
30-minute passenger trips into the tunnel, in glass-roofed boat with specialist guide. 3-hr through trip only available 1st Sat of month.
T:01484 844298 / 01782 785703 (Nov-Mar)
www.standedge.co.uk
Marsden Shuttle
The Shuttle is run by volunteers from the Huddersfield Narrow Canal Society, and operates as a Water Taxi for the 12-min trip between Marsden Station and Standedge Tunnel. Sun/Bank Hols April to October.
T:01457 871800 www.huddersfieldcanal.com

Geese and grandeur

This north Staffordshire walk is as intriguing as it is scenic, with stories blowing in the wind at every turn of the canal. A map will tell you that Great Haywood is the T-junction where the Staffs & Worcs meets the Trent & Mersey, but more quintessentially it is where the North teeters on the Midlands and dialects mingle amongst boaters.

In the boating season it's a popular spot, almost guaranteed to be stem to stern mooring with plenty of canal life for the walker to soak up.

From the water, boaters' kettles boil, Sunday papers sprawl the decks and it's the sort of place where boaty paraphernalia and Brasso come out with pride; yet there's always posher polish wafting from Shugborough Hall, the ancestral home of the Earls of Lichfield.

The mansion dates back to 1693, exuding panache and royal connections over the landscape and history under every frill and doily. Patrick, the photographer, was its most famous guardian, until his death in 2005.

The towpath leads southwards along the Staffs & Worcs Canal, briefly curving into an unusually wide swell of water. The canal tries to fool you that it has become a lake - and the illusion is deliberate.

The story goes that in the 18th century, when the canal was being built, Clifford Thomas who occupied the once nearby Tixall Hall was unimpressed by the idea of a water-motorway ruining his views. He grumbled enough to force the canal company to widen the bit of canal he could see from his home.

Even though it seems odd to walkers today that our idyllic narrow canals were once perceived as ugly, the disguise at Tixall Wide is still a treat. Boaters love it too, and throughout the summer it's rare to find an empty mooring slot.

The whole walk is a haven for wildlife as the canal winds through a conservation area. If you're lucky, you might spot a heron or even the blue flash of a kingfisher. It's probably true that gaggles of geese don't usually get the cooing 'aahs and oohs' that glamorous birds and swans do, but if you catch the air display they put on around dawn and dusk, you'll understand how goosebumps got their name.

Great Haywood is a popular daytime spot for geese, so there's a chance of witnessing the hullabaloo of a mass landing or take-off and an arrow-shaped flight of geese flapping and honking through the sky. One of the natural wonders of the waterways. Not to miss.

An ancient packhorse bridge takes you over the River Trent, following in the footsteps of gentry and countless paupers before. Wildlife, nature, and aristocratic history all mill in the water, giving this walk special indefinable grace. When the walk is near its end, the choice is to stop off for a cup of Earl Grey at Shugborough Hall's café, or hotfoot it to the Clifford Arms pub for a pint of Black Sheep.

Highlight of the walk

It's rumoured that the listed bridge at Great Haywood canal junction is the most photographed bridge on the canals. It's also a popular mooring spot for narrowboats and home to one of Anglo Welsh's hireboat bases.

Did you know?

Essex Bridge and the bridge at Great Haywood Junction are both Scheduled Ancient Monuments, and the gardens and landscape around Shugborough Hall are Grade I registered. Great Haywood, Tixall and Shugborough are also all designated Conservation Areas.

Fascinating fact

Legend has it that the ladies of Shugborough Hall in the 18th century didn't relish the uncouth idea of riding their own horses across the narrow packhorse bridge, Essex Bridge, over the River Trent. So they had a new wider bridge built to carry them in carriages, dressed in all their finery, over the river to church in the village, a mere few yards away!

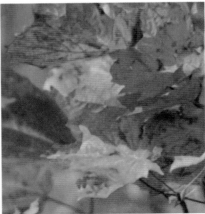

175

Start & Finish:
Great Haywood Junction
OS Grid ref: SJ994229
Distance:
4 miles approx
(circular walk)
Terrain:
Flat easy walking.
Towpath can get quite
muddy after rain.
OS Explorer Map - 244

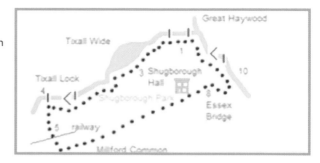

The walk - step by step

1. At the junction, follow the towpath opposite Anglo Welsh's hireboat base, crossing the small aqueduct over the River Trent (look out for kingfishers and heron along the river here).

2. Residential boats are moored on the opposite side of the canal and the towpath from here to Swivel Bridge is also popular mooring for visiting boats.

3. About a mile into the walk, the canal takes on the appearance of a lake as you arrive at Tixall Wide. This waterscape, still as a millpond in winter, transforms in the summer as boaters hog the idyllic moorings.

4. Continue round the Wide and the canal narrows again as it heads towards picturesque Tixall Lock, with its pretty lock cottage and gardens.

5. After a few hundred yards, pass bridge 106 then turn immediately left up steps to the road. Be wary of traffic.

6. Follow the road over the railway until you reach Milford Common. The entrance gate to the Shugborough Estate is on your left. Cannock Chase begins straight ahead.

7. Once in the estate, follow the road leading past Park Farm to Shugborough Hall. They have many rare breeds so don't be surprised by scary-looking horned cattle!

8. Just beyond the Hall is Essex Bridge, a packhorse bridge with low parapets and passing places, which crosses the River Trent again leading back to Great Haywood and the canal.

9. Cross the bridge and follow the road a few yards before turning right through a gateway towards the canal (continue straight on if you want to go into Great Haywood village).

10. Turn left on the towpath, continue under the bridge to Haywood Lock, and past visitors' moorings before reaching the junction again.

Where to eat

Lock House Restaurant
Great Haywood. Canalside by Haywood Lock.
T:01889 881294

Clifford Arms
Great Haywood (named after Clifford
Thomas). Short walk from Haywood Lock.
T:01889 881321

Fox & Hounds
Great Haywood. In the village, a short walk
from the canal.
T:01889 881252

Shugborough Hall
Lady Walk Tearoom & Restaurant and Ice
cream Shop: open daily from end March.
Farm Granary: open weekends and holidays
from end March.
T:01889 881388 www.shugborough.org.uk

Canalside Farm Shop
Great Haywood. Canalside near the junction.
Open daily 0900-1800 Apr-Oct. Winter opening
times vary. T:01889 881747

Best picnic spot
In the grounds of Shugborough Hall

Great Haywood
Choice of other pubs and cafés in Great
Haywood and Little Haywood.

Rawbones Meadow
Tixall. Alongside the canal at Tixall Wide,
the Meadow is a Site of Special Scientific
Interest (SSSI). It floods in winter and
maintains a high water table year round.
Home to a variety of nesting birds, and
specific water-loving flora.

Where to stay

Canalside B&Bs
Haywood Park Farm 4-star
Working farm, part of the
Shugborough Estate.
T:01889 882736
www.haywoodparkfarm.co.uk

High Meadows Guest House
Great Haywood. In the village,
a short walk from the canal.
T:01889 882449
www.highmeadowshouse.co.uk

Ye Old House
Wolseley Bridge. Near the
canal, a couple of miles beyond
Great Haywood.
T:01889 881264
www.yeoldhouse.co.uk

Canalside cottages
Tixall Gatehouse.
Overlooking Tixall Wide. Built
by Sir Walter Aston in the 16th
century, it's now owned by the
Landmark Trust. Dog-friendly.
T:01628 825925
www.landmarktrust.org.uk

And more
There's also a good choice of
self-catering, B&B and hotel
accommodation in and around
Stafford, Great Haywood &
Little Haywood.
www.visitstafford.org

How to get there

Train info
Nearest train station is Stafford
National Rail Enquiries T:08457 484950

Bus info
Traveline T:0871 2002233

Parking
Roadside in village or near canal

Local Tourist info

Stafford Tourist Information Centre
T:01785 619619 tic@staffordbc.gov.uk

Staffordshire & Worcestershire Canal Society
Established in 1959, the Society's mission is 'to protect and promote the Staffordshire & Worcestershire Canal (SWC) for the benefit and enjoyment of all'.
T:01380 721279 www.swcs.org.uk

Shugborough Hall
Shugborough is the UK's only complete working historic estate. It attracts visitors from all over the world to its restored working environments including working kitchens, dairy, water mill, brewhouse, walled garden and farm with rare breeds, all manned by guides dressed in historic costumes. The Hall is also the ancestral home to the Earls of Lichfield, most famous of which was Patrick, the photographer, who died in 2005, and his ancestor Admiral George Anson, who circumnavigated the globe in the 1740s.
Open daily 1100-1700 March to 29 October
T:01889 881388 www.shugborough.org.uk

Boats

Anglo Welsh Waterway Holidays
Great Haywood Junction.
Holiday & day boat hire.
T:0117 3041122 www.anglowelsh.co.uk

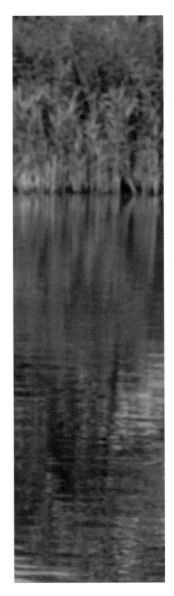

Peat and dry stone
Peak Forest Canal - Marple to Whaley Bridge

This canal is a brazen trespasser in some of England's hardiest walking territory – but the towpath along the Peak Forest Canal is easy underfoot so you don't have to be an experienced walker.

From the start at Marple Locks, views of the Peak Forest spread before you. Even though the landscape is remote, the canal never lets you feel lonely. And anyway, cheery Northern hellos are flung from passing boats and even the geese honk greetings that you could swear are friendly. Watch out for the herons around these parts too, they're so laid-back they trip you up on the towpath.

Marple Lock flight manages to be both good-looking and fascinating, as local stonework and history climb the flight with you. It's typical of canals to give you beauty to admire in one breath, and then grab you with fascinating heritage the next.

As well as admiring the locks themselves, near the top of the flight you'll find two tight tunnels carved into the hill at lock 13. This is sightseeing England's real history without 'keep out' barriers, or 'this way' banners. Walk through the tiny cobblestone tunnel, and you're inside a passage built for the horses that pulled working boats over two hundred years ago.

Don't just carry on walking though – look harder and you'll discover the second, even tinier, passage hiding by the lock side. It was for the boatmen working the lock and leads down to the bottom gates of the lock. If you get the chance to scramble into that dark spiralling passage and stand alone silently for a while, for that moment, you can live the everyday experience of a boat man in the great days of the 'canal mania'.

As you head off along the canal from Marple Locks, you're walking into a Peak District landscape softened by water. Bridges and leafiness mark the way. At first, heady whiffs of the countryside seep between trees lining the water but after tramping as far as bridge 28, the pong of manure is replaced by probably the sweetest smell on earth.

The smell of your childhood puffs from the Swizzle sweets factory on the canalside. The sugary smell powders onto your tongue and you're a child again, without a care in the world (try not to break into a skip, or get too near the edge of the water though).

The green miles ahead help you to grow up again, and then as you approach Whaley Bridge, where live-aboard boats occupy long term moorings, it's hard not to enjoy being secretly nosey as you pass (even if you know you shouldn't).

You'll reach the end of the walk with every emotion exhausted, so relax on the edge of the Peak District National Park pottering around Whaley Bridge.

Go window shopping, rest your legs in a teashop or pop to the pub.

Highlight of the walk

A flight of 16 locks heads away from Marple through woods towards Marple Aqueduct. Both the lock flight and the aqueduct are Grade I-listed, and the locks are among the deepest in the country, each lock rising 13 feet. The 300ft-long aqueduct took nearly 7 years to complete and stands over 100ft above the River Goyt below.

Did you know?

Bugsworth Basin, the original end of the canal, used to be an important busy terminus with boats loading stone brought down from the hills by tramway. It's an interesting detour along what is now the branch line to see the restored basin complex.

Fascinating fact

Possett Bridge by lock 13 acquired its name because Samuel Oldknow, a local industrialist and promoter of the canal, was anxious that the canal should be finished on time. To spur on the workmen, he had 'ale possetts' (hot milk, ale, bread & spice) made for their breakfast by nearby Navigation Inn. It must have worked: the canal was completed in time for Oldknow's boat to make the first trip through the locks.

Start:

Marple Aqudeuct
OS Grid ref: SJ951901

Finish:

Whaley Bridge
OS Grid ref: SK011816

Distance:

7 miles approx

Terrain:

Flat easy walking. Hilly
up the locks. Muddy in
rural parts after rain.

OS Explorer - 277/OL1

The walk - step by step

1. Join the towpath just above the Aqueduct near Romiley station.

2. Marple Aqueduct is almost overshadowed by the railway viaduct alongside. The scenery is dramatic with wooded views over the river Goyt.

3. Almost immediately Marple Locks flight begins. The woodland surroundings make the lower part of the flight an oasis of calm with just occasional glimpses of houses beyond

4. Cross the road at bridge 17 where the towpath changes sides. Look out for Samuel Oldknow's warehouse by lock 9, and what is believed to be a former tollhouse by lock 10.

5. Above lock 12, the canal widens. This used to be the site of a busy coal wharf, aptly named Black Wharf.

6. Look out for the intriguing tunnels under Possett Bridge, by lock 13. The last few locks have more open views down over the flight and, just

beyond Top Lock, you reach Marple Junction where the Macclesfield Canal heads off to the right.

7. Cross over the bridge at the entrance to the Macclesfield, and continue along the towpath opposite Top Lock House (originally built by Samuel Oldknow), the boatyard and stunning views over the Peak District. The canal heads out into open countryside with just a few houses by bridge 21 to disturb the scenery.

8. The first of two lift bridges (no.22) then the towpath is tarmacked between bridges 23 & 24, allowing access to the house by bridge 23.

9. A swing bridge (no.25) marks the start of the village of Disley, then back into rural surroundings until the warehouses and boats of New Mills come into view near bridge 28.

10. Pass the marina of Furness Vale spreading from bridge 30, then cross the original main line to Buxworth and continue into Whaley Bridge where the canal (and walk) terminates.

Where to eat

Ring O' Bells
Marple Junction. Canalside by bridge 2 of the Macclesfield Canal.
T:0161 4272300 www.ringobellsmarple.co.uk

The Navigation
Marple. Near lock 13.
T:0161 4273817

The Beehive
New Mills. Short walk from bridge 28.
T:01663 742087

The Crossings
Furness Vale. By the level crossing above bridge 31. T:01663 743642
www.thecrossingspub.com

The Dog & Partridge
Whaley Bridge. Over the footbridge (no.34)
T:01663 732284

Navigation Inn
Buxworth. Overlooking Bugsworth Basin at the end of the original main line.
T:01663 732072 www.navigationinn.co.uk

The Railway
Whaley Bridge. By the station, a short walk from the canal terminus.
T:01663 732245

Goyt Inn
Whaley Bridge. A short walk from the canal terminus.
T:01663 732840

Best picnic spot
Between bridges 29 and 30.

And more
Large choice of other pubs and cafés in Marple and Whaley Bridge.

Where to stay

Canalside B&Bs
The Grey Cottage 4-star
Disley. In the village, a short walk from the canal.
T:01663 763286
www.greycottagedisley.co.uk

Springbank Guest House 4-star
Whaley Bridge. Short walk from the canal terminus.
T:01663 732819
www.whaleyspringbank.co.uk

Canalside cottages
The White Cottage 3-star
Furness Vale. Canalside near the marina. Dog-friendly.
T:0845 2681553

Top Lock Bungalow 2-star
Marple. Canalside by the marina at Marple Junction. Dog-friendly. Wheelchair access. T:0845 6446332
www.toplocktraining.co.uk

Canalside hotels
Springfield Hotel
Marple. A short walk from the lock flight. T:0161 4490721
springfieldhotelmarple.co.uk

Best Western Moorside Grange Hotel, Higher Disley. About a mile from the canal. Dog-friendly. Wheelchair access.
T:01663 764151
www.moorsidegrangehotel.com

And more
Good choice of self-catering, B&B and hotel accommodation in and around Disley, Marple, New Mills and Whaley Bridge.
www.visitpeakdistrict.com

How to get there

Train info
Romiley, Marple, New Mills, Disley & Whaley Bridge.
National Rail Enquiries T:08457 484950

Bus info
Traveline T:0871 2002233

Parking
Roadside

Local Tourist info

Tourist Information Centre
Nearest is Buxton. T:01298 25106
tourism@highpeak.gov.uk
www.visitpeakdistrict.com

Marple Locks Heritage Society
Works in partnership with British Waterways to promote and enhance the flight. The Society also organises the Marple Locks Festival every other year.
T:0161 4270803 www.marplelocks.org.uk

Marple Lock Flight
A virtual tour of the lock flight with points of interest along the way.
www.marple-uk.com

Bugsworth Basin
The Basin has been restored thanks to efforts over 3 decades by volunteers of the Inland Waterways Protection Society (IWPS).
www.brocross.com/iwps

Boats

Judith Mary II
Whaley Bridge. Restaurant boat. Charter trips also available. T:01663 732408

Phoenix
Whaley Bridge. Day boat hire.
T:01663 747808
www.trafalgarmarineservices.co.uk

World Heritage heights
Llangollen Canal - Llangollen to Chirk

This walk forces everyone, no matter how many times they've been here before, to stand and stare, and surely ranks in the very best walks of Britain.

Every canal has its own highlight, but the Llangollen Canal has the Pontcysyllte Aqueduct - one of the official Seven Wonders of the Waterways. Pontcysyllte Aqueduct is only for adrenalin junkies. An inspirational feat of engineering that sends shivers to the vertiginous and the non-vertiginous. Believe it, or not, its 18 arches held together with ox blood and Welsh flannel have ridiculously kept the Llangollen Canal in flight above the River Dee for over 200 years.

The brave can tread the slim towpath that hugs the water, and gasp over sheer drops either side, but beware of pondering midway in case doubts set in. How can 127 feet of fresh air make narrowboats fly and a canal defy gravity?

A bit like the fisherman in the pub at the end of the day, it's hard not to rave about the 'Big One' but, as well as the marvel of the Aqueduct, the Llangollen Canal has plenty of other pleasures for the walker.

Beyond the short elastic of the car park in the sightseers' zone, walkers can step into remote Wales by canal towpath.

It's as solitary as it should be, and you only have to share your space with sheep, herons, soaring kite and the occasional narrowboat. Come in July and the towpath is even serenaded by heavenly choruses blowing in the breeze from Llangollen's annual Eisteddfod. The whole of Llangollen is singing. It's the law of physics of course that make the sounds of music travel far over water, but then it's the spirit of the waterways that makes them even sweeter.

The equally romantic sound of horses clopping rhythmically down the towpath is another rare pleasure that can be enjoyed on the Llangollen Canal. Horseboating is a seriously exciting part of the living history of the canals, and there are only a handful of commercial operators keeping the traditional skills alive.

There's a lot to see and absorb on this canal, but try to fit in time to see Horseshoe Falls, a semi-circular weir created by Thomas Telford to provide water for the canal.

Then there's the marvel of Telford's Chirk Aqueduct, half in England and half in Wales. The aqueduct was built in the late 1700s and is 70ft high, with ten spans taking the canal over the river Ceiriog. The unexpected drama of the aqueduct is the presence of the railway viaduct running alongside, 30ft higher than the canal (canal and railway enthusiasts can brush side by side).

Wildlife, water, heritage, boats, amazing engineering marvels and music. The Llangollen Canal has too much to take in on one day, so stay for the weekend, or come back again as soon as you can.

DOG MOORING

Highlight of the walk

Pontcysyllte Aqueduct is the longest and highest in the UK. Built by William Jessop and Thomas Telford, it is considered to be one of Telford's greatest engineering achievements. The aqueduct and 18km of canal were awarded World Heritage Site status in 2009.

Did you know?

Llangollen officially has the status of a 'Walkers are Welcome' town. One of the National Trails, the long-distance Offa's Dyke Path joins the Llangollen Canal towpath at bridge 27 just outside Chirk, then crosses Pontcysyllte Aqueduct before it heads back up into the surrounding hills.

www.walkersarewelcome.org.uk
www.nationaltrail.co.uk

Fascinating fact

Held every July for the past 60 years, Llangollen's International Music Eisteddfod is one of the world's greatest music festivals. With musicians and dancers from over 50 countries, there are daily music and dance competitions, and spectacular evening concerts.

6-11 July 2010 www.llangollen2010.co.uk
www.llangollen.org.uk

Start:
Llangollen Wharf
OS Grid ref: SJ214422
Finish:
Chirk
OS Grid ref: SJ297370
Distance:
9 miles approx
Terrain:
Flat easy walking. Muddy
in rural parts after rain.
OS Explorer Map
- 256/240

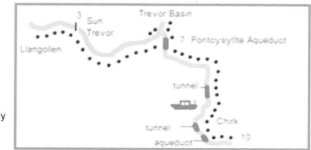

The walk - step by step

1. At Llangollen Wharf, if you have time, follow the horse-drawn boats left along the canal towards its end near Horseshoe Falls. Otherwide turn right to follow the towpath out of town.

2. The canal is very narrow, often only wide enough for one boat but, once you're past the visitors' moorings, both canal and towpath widen as glorious views spread out in front of you.

3. Passing the lift bridge, the canal curves under bridge 42, then the trees clear and the view of the Dee valley below is breathtaking.

4. Views of the valley and the ruins of Castell Dinas Bran on the hill behind you, but also a birds-eye-view of boats slowly wending their way through this narrow passage.

5. Once you've dragged yourself away from the view, and past the Sun Trevor pub above bridge 41, the canal continues to wind its narrow way past

sheep-filled fields, trees and under pretty stone bridges, until you arrive at the edge of Trevor Basin.

6. Here cross a narrow footbridge over the canal, past some houses then cross over the road to the gate to the Basin. Anglo Welsh's base and café/shop are on your left, and the magnificent Pontcysyllte Aqueduct awaits you to the right.

7. Cross the footbridge over the basin and turn right to walk over the Aqueduct - a vertiginous experience.

8. Past the swing bridge, there are views back across the valley to the Aqueduct. Follow the towpath until it meets the road at bridge 27 before heading south towards Chirk.

9. Chirk Marina is beyond Whitehouse Tunnel then, after a short wooded stretch, walk through Chirk Tunnel. You emerge to the view of Chirk Aqueduct with the railway viaduct alongside. Walk over the aqueduct then retrace your steps to the station.

Where to eat

Wharf Tea Room & Gift shop
Llangollen Wharf. Open daily Mar-October. Weekends rest of the year. T:01978 860702 www.horsedrawnboats.co.uk/wharf.asp

The Sun Trevor
Sun Bank. Overlooking the canal at bridge 41. T:01978 860651 www.suntrevor.co.uk

Telford Inn
Trevor Basin. Canalside. T:01978 820469

Aqueduct Inn
Froncysyllte. Above canal with views towards Pontcysyllte Aqueduct. T:01691 772481

The Hand Hotel
Chirk. Near the station, short walk from canal. T:01691 773472 www.thehandhotelchirk.co.uk

The Bridge Inn
Chirk Bank. Overlooking Chirk Aqueduct. T:01691 773213

Poachers Pocket
Chirk. Canalside near bridge 19. T:01691 773250

Best picnic spot
Just beyond bridge 42 overlooking the Dee valley (or on the grass next to Pontcysyllte).

Llangollen
Large choice of other pubs and cafés in Llangollen and Chirk.

Plas Newydd
Llangollen. The perfectly preserved Gothic-style home of the 'Ladies of Llangollen' Open Easter-Oct 1000-1700. T:01978 861314 www.llangollen.com/plas

Llangollen Motor Museum & canal exhibition
Pentrefelin. Canalside by bridge 48. Open daily March to October 1000-1700. Winter opening by arrangement. T:01978 860324 www.llangollenmotormuseum.co.uk

Where to stay

Canalside B&Bs
Borrows Rest 3-star Trevor. Overlooks Pontcysyllte Aqueduct. T:01978 822933

Bryn Meirion 4-star Llangollen. Canalside. T:01978 861911

Glencoed 3-star Pentre. Canalside near Aqueduct. T:01691 778148 www.glencoed.co.uk

Ty Camlas 3-star Near Llangollen Wharf. (2-bed flat) T:01978 861969 www.tycamlas.co.uk

Canalside campsites
Wern Isaf Campsite Llangollen. ½-mile walk from the Wharf. T:01978 860632

Lady Margaret's Park Caravan Club Site. Chirk. Short walk from Chirk Tunnel. T:01691 777200 www.caravanclub.co.uk

Canalside cottages
Dock House Trevor Basin. Near Pontcysyllte Aqueduct. T:0117 3041122 www.anglowelsh.co.uk

Canalside hotels
Chainbridge Hotel 3-star Llangollen. Near Horseshoe Falls. T:01978 860215 www.chainbridgehotel.com

Bryn Howel Hotel 3-star Canalside near bridge 38. T:01978 860331 www.brynhowel.com

The Hand Hotel Chirk. Near the station, a short walk from Chirk Tunnel. T:01691 773472 www.thehandhotelchirk.co.uk

And more
Choice of self-catering, B&Bs and hotels in and around Chirk & Llangollen. www.chirk.com & www.llangollen.org.uk

How to get there

Train info
Nearest train station is Chirk
National Rail Enquiries T:08457 484950

Bus info
Traveline Cymru T:0871 2002233

Parking
Roadside or public car parks

Local Tourist info

Llangollen Tourist Information Centre
T:01978 860828 llangollen@nwtic.com

Llangollen Steam Railway
Runs from Llangollen for 7½ miles along the river Dee. T:01978 860979
www.llangollen-railway.co.uk

Chirk Castle
1½ miles from Chirk Tunnel. Open most of week Feb-Nov. Check website for variations. T:01691 777701 www.nationaltrust.org.uk

Boats

Anglo Welsh Waterway Holidays
Trevor Basin. Holiday & day boat hire.
T:0117 3041122 www.anglowelsh.co.uk

Black Prince Narrowboat Holidays
Chirk Marina. Holiday boat hire.
T:01527 575115 www.black-prince.com

Crest Narrowboats
Chirk Marina. Holiday boat hire.
T:01691 774558 www.crestnarrowboats.co.uk

Horse-drawn boat trips
Llangollen Wharf. Daily Easter to October.
T:01978 860702 www.horsedrawnboats.co.uk

Trips across Pontcysyllte Aqueduct:

'Thomas Telford'
Llangollen Wharf Twice daily Easter to October
T:01978 860702 www.horsedrawnboats.co.uk

'Eirlys', Jones the Boats
Trevor Basin. Public trips daily Easter to October. Charter trips also available.
T:01691 690322 www.canaltrip.co.uk

Mountain air

Towpath walks usually treat the walker to enough canal highlights to forgive any in-between mile of monotony, but the Mon & Brec spoils you with delicious scenery every step of the way. These spectacular waterways miles shouldn't be rushed: pack a rucksack and escape for the whole weekend if you can.

This is Welsh walking; a waterside trail in the company of mountains, sheep and open spaces, with the taste of real air to feed your boots. The canal sets off travelling through the heart of the Brecon Beacons National Park, and most of the route runs parallel to the river Usk.

Because it's not connected to Britain's main canal networks, the slow waters of the Mon & Brec miss the boaty buzz of through traffic yet gain more on intimacy and calm cruising.

The towpath seems to hide from the worries of the world under a canopy of trees for part of this walk, with mountainous peaks and Pen y Fan yelling ahead. No matter how grateful you are for each waterways mile, just when you think the views couldn't get any better, they do.

You're spoilt for choice for picnic spots but Ty Newydd is definitely a place to pull out your flask and soak up the view.

Despite being a high hill trail, the towpath from Brecon is easily accessible and its kind nature makes it popular with sunny-day strollers and extreme outdoor enthusiasts alike. But walkers who prefer solitude shouldn't be too upset, especially if you avoid Bank Holiday weekends.

This isn't a canal walk for lock enthusiasts since most of the way is lock free, but Brynich Lock makes up for the lack of numbers by winning awards for its fabulous displays of flowers.

Other features of interest include several lift bridges and Brynich Aqueduct. Built by the engineer Thomas Dadford, the the four-arched aqueduct elegantly carries the canal over the River Usk below.

The cheekiest reward of this walk is that while scramblers knuckle their way to the summits of Pen y Fan and other surrounding heights, the Brecon Beacons are never more than an amble for the lucky towpath walker.

Highlight of the walk

The dramatic setting at Ty Newydd boatyard with the Brecon Beacons as a backdrop. Pen y Fan stands majestically in the distance and there are 360° views of the surrounding scenery.

Did you know?

The Taff Trail Cycle Route follows the Mon & Brec Canal from just outside Brecon to Brynich Lock where cyclists head off on the road, though walkers on the Trail can continue on the canal as far as Talybont-on-Usk.

www.tafftrail.org.uk

Fascinating fact

Spot the rusting diamond-shaped signposts (some now painted in black & white - see page 245) peeping over many stone bridges on the Mon & Brec. A world without cars seems inconceivable today, yet of course canals preceded our carbon-burning noise polluters. With the arrival of the motor car, new pressure was put on canal bridges originally constructed for foot passengers or horse & cart. These signs warned drivers of new-fangled motors to beware of the weight limit (up to 5 tons!)

Start:
Brecon Basin
OS Grid ref: SO046281
Finish:
Talybont-on-Usk
OS Grid ref: SO111229
Distance:
6 miles approx
Terrain:
Flat easy walking. Muddy in rural parts after rain.
OS Explorer Map
- OL12/13

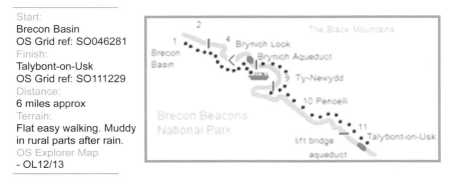

The walk - step by step

1. In Brecon Basin, head down to the canal in front of the Theatr Brycheiniog and follow the towpath under Dadford's Bridge.

2. As you head beyond bridge 166, the canal surroundings take on the feel of a linear park.

3. Pass Watton Bridge and go over the wooden stile or through the gate. To the right, there are open country views down to the River Usk and across to the mountains.

4. Just beyond bridge 164, there's a conveniently placed bench with its back to the canal, facing one of the best views on the canal network.

5. The canal becomes tree-lined on both sides until you reach the award-winning Brynich Lock, with its pretty lock house and flowers.

6. Go through the gate and cross the road (a detour to the right takes you to the bridge over the river Usk).

7. Just around the corner from the lock, the towpath crosses Thomas Dadford's Brynich Aqueduct, one of many on this canal but the most notable as it carries the canal over the River Usk below.

8. Pass the popular moorings beyond the aqueduct, then go through the gate and over the bridge to continue on the opposite side of the canal.

9. You emerge from a short wooded stretch to the glorious setting of Cambrian Cruisers' boatyard at Ty Newydd, overlooked by the National Park's highest peak, Pen y Fan.

10. The canal loops round through woods until it reaches Pencelli and the first of the canal's lift bridges.

11. Past the Royal Oak, the canal bends round to a wooded stretch with 3 more lift bridges in quick succession. The road lift bridge marks your arrival into Talybont-on-Usk.

Where to eat

Tipple 'n' Tiffin
Brecon. In the Theatr Brycheiniog, canalside in Brecon Basin.
T:01874 611866 www.brycheiniog.co.uk

White Swan
Llanfrynach. Short walk from bridge 157.
T:01874 665276 www.the-white-swan.com

Royal Oak
Pencelli. Canalside by bridge 153.
T:01874 665396

Travellers Rest
Talybont-on-Usk. Canalside by bridge 142.
T:01874 676233
www.travellersrestinn.com

White Hart Inn & Bunkhouse
Talybont-on-Usk. Canalside by bridge 143.
T:01874 676227
www.breconbunkhouse.co.uk

Star Inn
Talybont-on-Usk. Canalside by the aqueduct.
(Photos inside the pub show the extent of damage caused when the nearby aqueduct flooded it in 1994)
T:01874 676635 www.starinntalybont.co.uk

Best picnic spot
Ty Newydd with its open views of Pen y Fan.

Brecon & Talybont
Large choice of other pubs and cafés in Brecon and Talybont.

Working boats
The Mon & Brec Canal was once busy with boat traffic, carrying cargoes of iron and coal. Traditional working boats in the Midlands had to have the whole family living (and working) on board, but on the Mon & Brec only men crewed the boats, going home after work.

Where to stay

Canalside B&Bs
Canal Bank 5-star
Brecon. Canalside near Watton Bridge. T:01874 623464
www.accommodation-breconbeacons.co.uk

Canalside campsites
Brynich Caravan Club Site
Brecon. Short walk from bridge 164. T:01874 623325
www.caravanclub.co.uk

Pencelli Castle Caravan & Camping Park 5-star. Near bridge 153. T:01874 665451
www.pencelli-castle.com

Gilestone Caravan Park 4-star
Talybont-on-Usk. Short walk from canal. T:01874 676236
ww.gilestonecaravanpark.co.uk

Canalside cottages
Darnley Cottage 4-star
Pencelli. Short walk from canal. Dog-friendly. T:01873 810811
www.wiseinwales.co.uk

The Briars 4-star
Pencelli. Short walk from canal. Counting House 2-star
Talybont-on-Usk. Grade 11-listed Canalside Toll House. Glan Camlas Cottage 3-star
Talybont-on-Usk. Canalside. Above three - T:01874 676446
www.breconcottages.com

Canalside pubs & inns
Star Inn, Talybont-on-Usk. Canalside by aqueduct.
T:01874 676635
www.starinntalybont.co.uk

Travellers Rest
Talybont-on-Usk. Canalside by bridge 142. T:01874 676233
www.travellersrestinn.com

And more
Good choice of self-catering, B&Bs and hotels in and around Brecon and Talybont.
breconbeaconstourism.co.uk

How to get there

Train info
Nearest station is Abergavenny
National Rail Enquiries T:08457 484950

Bus info
Traveline Cymru T:0871 2002233

Parking
Car park by Brecon Basin (charge) or roadside

Local Tourist info

Tourist Information Centre
Brecon. T:01874 622485
www.breconbeaconstourism.co.uk

Beacons Bus
A great way to combine walking on the canal
and the Beacons. Walk one way then get the
bus back. T:01873 853254

Brecon Beacons National Park
T:01874 624437
www.breconbeacons.org

Theatr Brycheiniog (Brecon Theatre)
Canal Wharf, Brecon T:01874 611622

Monmouthshire, Brecon & Abergavenny
Canals Trust.
Established in 1984, the Trust
aims to promote and restore the entire length
of the canal. T:01633 892167
www.mon-brec-canal-trust.org.uk

Boats

Dragonfly Cruises
Brecon Basin. 2½-hour boat cruises from
Brecon to Brynich. Timings and days vary.
Wheelchair access. T:07831 685222
www.dragonfly-cruises.co.uk

Beacon Park Day Boats
Brecon Basin. Day boat hire and Canadian
canoes. Includes expert tuition. T:0800
6122890 www.beaconparkdayboats.co.uk

Cambrian Cruisers
Ty Newydd. Holiday boat hire.
T:01874 665315 www.cambriancruisers.co.uk

Brecon Boats
Talybont. Day boat hire. T:01874 676401

Limekilns and leaves

It's no wonder Brecon is thought of as the outdoor capital of Wales for cycling, hiking, scrambling, kayaking, caving, pony trekking and more. Bright-eyed healthy adventurers who love pumping their lungs are drawn to the best parts of Wales for outdoor pursuits.

And the Brecon Beacons National Park describes itself as the place "where the skyscrapers are mountains and the only traffic is sheep, hikers and the odd mountain pony".

The Monmouthshire & Brecon Canal runs through the heart of the National Park, but you won't find it bragging about its treasures. That's not the way of canals. This Welsh canal is a secret hideaway with intimate rewards.

And this walk from Llanfoist to Llangynidr follows a section of the canal that is even less trodden than the more noticed towpath nearer the geared-up crowds of Brecon.

There are big views with mountains, cormorants, red kites, sheep and rolls of Welsh grass – but tree huggers get ready, because this is your sort of walk. Canopies in greens to ochres throughout the seasons, with leaves shading the sun in summer and surfing the water in autumn. Look out for the giant Redwood with a trunk so huge you can't stretch even halfway round in a hug.

The whole route is a quiet commune with nature, but it's not just that. The remains of kilns and tramways remind the explorer of times when coal, iron and limestone were brought from the hills to be transported by canal.

The boats on the water are for leisure today and don't have to worry about industrial cargo, but the canal is still all about the boats. Even the walker gets over-excited when a narrowboat cruises by, seeming in no hurry to get anywhere soon.

Many of the boats on the isolated Mon & Brec are shorter than narrowboats on the main canal networks of Britain; and the land-locked waterway has a village culture without the buzz of canal travellers that pass through on their way elsewhere.

The Mon & Brec Canal is remote. But does the word remote imply something is missing? Perhaps the noise of roads, clocks ticking, jobs, chores and the mean tricks of material life.

Thank goodness this walk is a purifying escape that fills you up with absolutely nothing.

Highlight of the walk

Llangynidr's lock flight is full of contrasts. At busy times there's a holiday hustle and bustle, particularly around the bottom lock (and the convenient moorings just above it) and by the pub beyond. Then the rest of the flight is left calmer as the locks lead up through trees to idyllic moorings.

Did you know?

The Monmouthshire & Brecon Canal was originally two separate canals - the Monmouthshire Canal and the Brecknock & Abergavenny Canal - the two were linked at Pontymoile. Today's navigable 'Mon & Brec' is mostly the former Brecknock & Abergavenny.

Fascinating fact

The wharves and canal at both Llanfoist and Govilon form part of the Blaenavon Industrial Landscape World Heritage Site. At the height of the Industrial Revolution, iron and coal were transported from the ironworks at Blaenavon along horse-operated tramroads down to the canal where they were stored in canalside warehouses before being loaded onto canal boats.

www.world-heritage-blaenavon.org.uk

Start:
Llanfoist Wharf
OS Grid ref: SO284130
Finish:
Llangynidr
OS Grid ref: SO145198
Distance:
12 miles approx
Terrain:
Flat easy walking. Hilly up locks. Muddy in rural parts after rain.
OS Explorer Map - OL13

The walk - step by step

1. Turn right onto the towpath opposite the picturesque base of Beacon Park Boats in the old wharf at Llanfoist.

2. The canal follows a wooded cutting before the towpath crosses sides at bridge 97 on the outskirts of Govilon.

3. Just beyond bridge 97, lines of moored boats indicate your arrival at Govilon Boat Club and Bailey's Warehouse at the former terminus of the tramroad from Nantyglo Ironworks.

4. The towpath crosses sides again over the pretty wooden bridge (no.98) before heading into another wooded stretch before the main 'Heads of the Valley' road noisily encroaches.

5. Once under the main road at bridge 102 and round the corner, peace is restored as you approach Gilwern.

6. At the end of the busy village, with its boatyard and pubs, go through the wooden gate just after a picnic area.

7. Disappearing into the trees again, the canal opens out into glorious views by bridge 110.

8. Look out for the huge Redwood tree just beyond bridge 113.

9. Moored boats surround the historic buildings and limekilns at Llangattock wharf. Limestone was brought down by tramroad from the quarries above then loaded onto canal boats.

10. Crickhowell town is just across the Usk valley and the canal is once again engulfed by trees with occasional glimpses of stunning scenery beyond.

11. Just past Llangynidr's first lock, the canal swoops round two bends, past a well-positioned pub garden, before climbing the last four locks which are surrounded by trees.

12. Beyond Top Lock, there are more popular moorings and a picnic area. The choice now is to continue another two miles to Talybont-on-Usk, or catch the (infrequent!) bus to Abergavenny.

Where to eat

The Old Rectory Country Hotel
Llangattock. Short walk from bridges 116/117 (its grounds border the canal).
T:01873 810373 www.rectoryhotel.co.uk

The Horse Shoe Inn
Llangattock. In the village, a short walk from the canal.
T:01873 810393

The Bridge End
Govilon. In the village, a short walk from bridge 98. T:01873 830939

Bridgend Inn
Gilwern. Canalside by bridge 103.
T:01873 830939

Navigation Inn
Gilwern. Canalside by bridge 103.
T:01873 832015

The Beaufort Arms
Gilwern. Short walk from bridge 103.
T:01873 832235 www.beaufortarms.co.uk

Corn Exchange
Gilwern. In the village, a short walk from the canal. T:01873 830337

Coach & Horses
Llangynidr. Canalside by bridge 133.
T:01874 730245
www.coachandhorses.org

Red Lion Hotel
Llangynidr. Short walk from bridge 129.
T:01873 730223

Best picnic spot
Between bridges 110 & 111, or 120 & 121.

Abergavenny & Crickhowell
Large choice of other pubs and cafés in & around Abergavenny and Crickhowell.

Where to stay

Canalside campsites
Park Farm Caravan & Camping
Llangattock. Short walk from bridge 112. T:01873 812183

Cwrt-Isaf Farm
Llangattock. Short walk from bridge 118. T:01873 812128
www.cwrt-isaf.co.uk

Riverside Caravan & Camping
Crickhowell. By the river about a mile from the canal.
T:01873 810397
riversidecaravanscrickhowell.co.uk

Canalside cottages
Courtyard Cottage 4-star
Hopyard Farm, Govilon. Near bridge 100. Wheelchair access.
T:01873 830219
hopyardcourtyardcottage.co.uk

The Neuadd Holiday cottages
Llangattock. A short walk from bridge 115. T:01873 810244
www.theneuadd.co.uk

Hengwaithdy 4-star
Crickhowell. Overlooking canal near bridge 118. Dog-friendly.
T:01873 810811
www.wiseinwales.co.uk

Canalside hotels
The Old Rectory Country Hotel
Llangattock. Short walk from bridges 116/117. T:01873 810373 www.rectoryhotel.co.uk

Canalside pubs & inns
The Beaufort Arms 3-star
Gilwern. Short walk from bridge 103. T:01873 832235
www.beaufortarms.co.uk

Coach & Horses
Llangynidr. Canalside by bridge 133. T:01874 730245
www.coachandhorses.org

And more
Good choice of self-catering, B&Bs and hotels in and around Abergavenny and Crickhowell.
www.visitabergavenny.co.uk
www.crickhowellinfo.org.uk

How to get there

Train info
Abergavenny
National Rail Enquiries T:08457 484950
Bus info
Traveline Cymru T:0871 2002233
Parking
Several car parks to choose from in
Abergavenny, or roadside

Local Tourist info

Tourist Information Centre
Abergavenny. T:01873 853254
abergavennyic@breconbeacons.org
www.breconbeaconstourism.co.uk
Brecon Beacons National Park
T:01874 624437
www.breconbeacons.org
Monmouthshire, Brecon & Abergavenny
Canals Trust. Established in 1984, the Trust
aims to promote and restore the entire length
of the canal. T:01633 892167
www.mon-brec-canal-trust.org.uk

Boats

Beacon Park Boats
Llanfoist Wharf. Holiday boat hire.
T:01873 858277
www.beaconparkboats.com
Castle Narrowboats
Gilwern. Holiday boat hire.
T:01873 830001 www.castlenarrowboats.co.uk
Road House Narrowboats
Gilwern. Holiday boat hire.
T:01873 830240
www.narrowboats-wales.co.uk
Country Craft Narrowboats
Llangynidr. Holiday boat hire.
T:01874 730850
www.countrycraftnarrowboats.co.uk

The wild Highlands
Caledonian Canal - Corpach to Gairlochy

It's wild, it's woolly and it's non-negotiably wonderful. Between the
crunching of your boots on the towpath, you can (if you try hard enough)
hear the cries of clans and squeals of mournful bagpipes swirling the
peaks of this highland landscape. The water keeps you looking ahead but
the Highlands play with your mind: a fickle sweep of light can turn joyous
mountains into a dark looming menace - then in another single puff of
weather let you breath again.

Ben Nevis, the highest mountain in Britain, looks down over the outskirts
of Fort William; and as you trundle away from town, following the edge
of Loch Linnhe, you reach Corpach Basin at the start of the Caledonian
Canal. Here, the life of the water takes its grip and digs goosebumps out
of your skin. Anywhere you've ever walked before, or are yet to walk,
blanks from your mind as this place wills you to stand still for a while,
trapped in one moment. A giant double lock marks the start of the canal
and the Highlands call. Pull on a pom-pom hat and prepare for high air;
but don't worry if you're not an experienced walker because even though
this towpath leads you into real hiking territory, it's miraculously an easy
walk. You can meet all sorts of walkers on the Caledonian towpath, and
everyone's got one thing in common – so don't even think of passing

another walker without saying good morning and meaning it.

The first flight of locks is dependably spectacular. Neptune's Staircase doesn't even pretend to be as modest as those on narow canals south of the borders. Huge chambers and lock gates carry boats up into the Highlands with every fluid ounce of drama you'd expect.

Before the canal was built, boats had to navigate the ferocious sea of the north coast to travel from the west side of Scotland to the east, and there were no roads to make a highland pasage any easier either. The Great Glen and its lochs and rivers gave Thomas Telford, a Scotsman, the starting point for his radical project of building Scotland's coast to coast canal in the Highlands.

The canal opened in 1822 during the time of the Highland clearances. Crofters were forced to abandon their farms, migrating to towns, less fertile land or emigrating to America. Highland history is fiery and politically contentious, blighted by famine, cholera, the banning of wearing tartan kilts and restrictions on drinking whisky. The Caledonian Canal brought employment during troubled times of poverty and disruption. It was built by navvies whose blood was notoriously fuelled on whisky and whose labour leaves its legacy virtually untouched by progress today for tourists, boaters and walkers to respect.

Holly, gorse, birch, fern and heather remind you the walk isn't only about the canal and the show-grabbing mountains. The smell of pine trees and bright red berries of Rowan trees vie sweetly for attention. The deeper you venture into the Highlands, the more your route erases distant disturbance in your subconcious of the madness of urban chaos and noisy cars. The Caledonian talks to you with its own convincing spirit and leaves you with a wild inner peace that lurks within until you can come back again. Glossy travel writers will say the Andes, Bernese Oberland, Bondi Beach are sublime destinations; walkers on the Caledonian Canal know another.

Highlight of the walk

The men who built the flight in the early 1800s gave the flight its name, Neptune, after the Roman God of the sea. If your timing's lucky, you might catch the morning or matinée performance of boats travelling through the locks with waterfalls thundering over lock gates as they fill and empty in rhythmic logic.

Did you know?

The law is different in Scotland from the rest of the UK - wild camping is permitted along the Caledonian, so long as you are of course responsible, leaving no trace.

Fascinating fact

Nature built the Great Glen around 400 million years ago when two land masses crashed together, causing mountains to erupt, giving the highlands and lowlands their relationship. It's Scotland's longest glen, over 60 miles linking west & east coasts. The Caledonian Canal was built in the 19th century to enable boats to avoid the risky sea journey around the north of Scotland, and the 77-mile Great Glen Way long-distance trail opened in 2002.

www.greatglenway.com

Start:
Corpach
OS Grid ref: NN095766
Finish:
Gairlochy
OS Grid ref: NN176842
Distance:
8 miles (11 from Fort W)
Terrain:
Flat easy walking. Good
surface.
OS Explorer Map
- 392/399

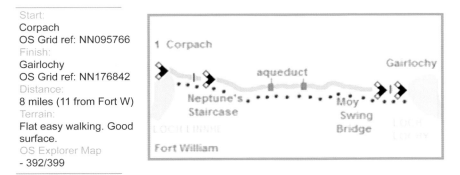

The walk - step by step

1. The official Great Glen Way starts in Fort William, 3 miles from the start of the canal, and takes you round the bay of Loch Linnhe to Corpach.

2. Our walk begins once you reach the spectacular basin at Corpach. The sea lock opens out to Loch Linnhe, and the backdrop of Ben Nevis is stunning.

3. Once you've explored the basin and British Waterways office, follow the towpath to the right of Double Lock.

4. There are glimpses of the houses of Caol to your right, but the view ahead is just greenery and mountains.

5. After just under a mile, you'll see the infamous Neptune's Staircase, a flight of locks heading uphill in front of you. Take care across the level crossing then over the road to reach the locks.

6. Allow some time to walk up the lock flight. There is so much to look at: the cavernous lock chambers, black and

white paintwork, old capstans, information boards, a tearoom and shop, a pub, not to mention the thrill of watching a boat helped through the locks by the keepers.

7. Once you tear yourself away from the bustle of the Staircase and past the large mooring area above, you are immediately surrounded by stunning Highland scenery of trees, hills, sheep and dramatic mountains.

8. After a sign to Shengain Aqueduct, then a pretty white cottage, you reach Loy sluices and Glen Loy Aqueduct, the biggest of four along this stretch. A 'Great Glen Ways' display board explains the importance of the area.

10. A mile or so further on, Moy swing bridge and cottage come into view. There are great views over the river Lochy to the Ben Nevis range on your right along the next mile or so.

11. The walk ends where the canal meets Loch Lochy at the locks and swing bridge at Gairlochy.

Where to eat

Moorings Hotel
Banavie. Canalside by Neptune's Staircase.
Dog-friendly. T:01397 772797
www.moorings-fortwilliam.co.uk

Telford Tearoom
Gairlochy. Canalside between Top Lock and
Loch Lochy. The former lock-keeper's house
dates from the time the first lock was built (the
second was added in 1844 after major floods),
and Telford used to stay here during his visits
to the canal. T:01397 713900

Best picnic spot
Between bridges 29 and 30.

And more
Large choice of other pubs and cafés in Fort
William, Corpach and Banavie.

Canoeing
Canoeing is extremely popular along the
Caledonian Canal and the Great Glen
Canoe Trail, Scotland's first official canoe
trail, is currently being developed.
Canoes or kayaks can be hired at:

Rhiw Goch
Mountain bike and Canadian canoe hire.
T:01397 772373 www.rhiwgoch.co.uk

Highland Activities
Organise outdoor activities including
canoeing and kayaking. T:0845 0945513
www.highlandactivities.co.uk

Moy Bridge
The only remaining original cast-iron
swing bridge on the Caledonian Canal.
Designed by Thomas Telford, each half
is opened and closed by hand from its
own side of the canal - so after opening
the bridge on the towpath side, the bridge
keeper then has to row across the canal
to open the other half.

Where to stay

Canalside B&Bs
Rhiw Goch, Banavie. Canalside
near Neptune's Staircase.
T:01397 772373
www.rhiwgoch.co.uk

Dalcomera
Gairlochy. Riverside, a short
walk from the canal. T:01397
712778 www.dalcomera.co.uk

Canalside campsites
Lochy Holiday Park
Fort William. Short walk from
Neptune's Staircase. Self-
catering also. T:01397 703446
www.lochy-holiday-park.co.uk

Gairlochy Holiday Park 4-star
Gairlochy. Short walk from the
canal. T:01397 712711
www.theghp.co.uk

Canalside cottages
Bank Cottage
Banavie. By Neptune's
Staircase. T:07812 849477
www.bankcottage.co.uk

Highland Lodges 3-star
South Laggan. By Loch Lochy.
Dog-friendly T:01809 501225
www.highlandlodges.org.uk

Canalside Apartments 5-star
Banavie. Next to Neptune's
Staircase. Wheelchair access.
Dog-friendly. T:07786966245
highlandholidayapartments.co.uk

Seangan Croft Lodges &
Cottages 3-star. Muirshearlich.
Canalside. Dog-friendly. T:0141
5890014 www.seangan.co.uk

Canalside hotels
Moorings Hotel 3-star
Banavie. Neptune's Staircase.
Dog-friendly. T:01397 772797
www.moorings-fortwilliam.co.uk

And more
Good choice of self-catering,
B&Bs and hotels in & near Fort
William, Banavie & Gairlochy.
www.visithighlands.com

How to get there

Train info

Corpach, Banavie, Fort William & Spean
Bridge www.scotrail.co.uk
National Rail Enquiries T:08457 484950

Bus info

Traveline Scotland T:0871 2002233

Parking

Roadside or various car parks to choose from

Local Tourist info

Information Centre Fort William

T:0845 2255121 info@visitscotland.com

British Waterways Scotland

For more information about the Caledonian
Canal. www.scottishcanals.co.uk

Clan Cameron Museum

On the banks of Loch Lochy, 2 miles beyond
Gairlochy. Explore the history of the clan with
artefacts, displays and clan records.
T:01397 712480 www.clan-cameron.org

West Highland steam train

'The Jacobite' runs from Fort William to Mallaig
(it crosses the canal at the foot of Neptune's
Staircase), following the route of Hogwarts
Express in the Harry Potter films.
T:0845 1284681 www.steamtrain.info

Boats

Caledonian Discovery Limited

Corpach. 'Fingal of Caledonia' is a converted
holiday barge cruising the Caledonian Canal.
T:01397 772167 www.fingal-cruising.co.uk

European Waterways

'Scottish Highlander' is a luxury barge cruising
the Caledonian Canal.
T:01784 482439 www.gobarging.com

Things to look out for

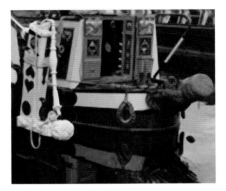

Wildlife

Canals are a haven for wildlife - a network of green corridors criss-cross the land with miles of hedgerows, trees, flowers and grasses. There are over 1,000 wildlife conservation sites and 65 Sites of Special Scientific Interest (SSSIs) along the canals.

Otters, kingfishers, ducks, swans, geese, moorhens, coots, herons, bats, frogs, snakes, dragonflies, foxes, badgers, damselflies, water voles and of course, fish.

Walk among wildflowers and butterflies on the water's edge. Tiptoe onto the towpaths at dawn and watch water life secretly waking, or go at dusk and you could bump into a bat or two under the bridges and trees.

To find your nearest canal, visit www.waterscape.com

Traditional narrowboats

Signwritten and decorated in the traditional colours of the canals...and adorned with beautifully functional rope fenders and knotwork, lacework and brass...

Roses & Castles

The traditional folk art of working boat families. A boatman's cabin and its paraphernalia would have been crudely daubed with brightly-coloured roses and castles. Canal folk art is still alive today, decorating pots and pans, planks and poles, and even souvenirs you can buy.

Dogs in traditional boat bandanas

Some are on holiday, and some live aboard narrowboat homes. And while waggy tails get all the fuss, there might be a quiet boat cat snoozing on the decks.

Mileposts

Every canal company had its own style of mileposts, lock numbers and lock name posts. Spot a milepost and the Industrial Revolution is looking you straight in the eye. The canals, built under Acts of Parliament, were required to have mileposts showing the working boatmen how far they had travelled and therefore how much they had to pay the canal companies who charged on a tonne and mile basis.

The mileposts' story doesn't stop with the Victorians; it goes on into World War II, telling the signspotter secret tales of national security. Many milestones were removed to prevent Nazi invaders mapping the country easily. Those signs that weren't lost or melted down for the war effort were put back after the war. But many had to wait years before local canal societies raised enough funds to replace them. To avoid confusion, new replica replacements are usually slightly altered from the originals.

Plaques

When you see a large collection of brass plaques, displayed on the back doors of a narrowboat, you'll know that the helmsman is well-travelled. Individual canals have their own emblem on a small brass plaque that boaters can collect once they've cruised a canal.

Hidden history

Aqueducts, tunnels and fancy engineering marvels are the obvious attractions for sightseers. But those who know where to look, will discover a historic story accidently written into the landscape by the daily life of ordinary boat families. If you look closely at the bricks on the underside of bridges, or the stonework on lock sides, you'll sometimes see gauged marks from the ropes that horses once towed heavy boats laden with cargo by. Some of the grooves are so deep you can run your fingers through and feel the daily sweat of those horses. There's something very special about touching history so intimately.

Stone masons' signatures

In the stonework of the canals, on aqueducts and bridges, you can sometimes see the signature of a stone mason if you look closely.

Datestones

Often secluded in the brickwork of canal structures.

Locks

Lock arms are painted in the uniform (and utterly seductive) black and white colours of British Waterways. They stretch out across the water giving Britain's canals their unique landscape. Some lock arms are metal but probably the most beautiful are wooden. Locks are operated simply by opening and shutting paddles at either end of a chamber to let water in or out.

How a lock works

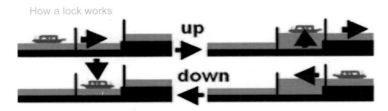

A million canal walks

Walk the longest canal in Britain

The Grand Union Canal - 137 miles from Birmingham to London.

Walk on water

Aqueducts are a feature of canal engineering, carrying canals over rivers and valleys. Follow the towpath over any aqueduct and it's a thrill, but only the brave should attempt the highest and longest of them all, the Pontcysyllte.

Walk in the city

Canals secretly tip-toe through cities and busy towns all across Britain. A leafy walk along an urban towpath isn't just a peaceful escape from the parallel frenzy, it's also a fascinating backdoor view. A place to make sense of it all!

Walk in circles

Canals link into a network, creating cruising rings. Some of the most popular are the Stourport Ring and the Cheshire Ring.
www.waterscape.com

Walk with boats

Mix it up for fun and hop on a boat for part of the day. Hire a day boat or go on a boat trip.

Walk for charity

Do it for fun and raise money for your favourite charity at the same time.

Walk with horses

Help keep canal traditions alive. Join the Horseboating Society.
www.horseboatingsociety.co.uk

Walk in the park

Because canals were originally built as trade routes, they nip in and out of the residential outskirts of towns and villages. Luckily, that means they've become perfect linear parks in many towns today. Take a stroll and feed the ducks.

Find your nearest canal
www.waterscape.com

Walk end to end across Britain by canal

Canals aren't only gentle strolls, they can be extreme walking too. Follow our end-to-end trail.
www.coolcanalsguides.com

Walk for food

Miles of hedgerows border the towpaths.Not just creating vital habitats for wildlife, but also bagfuls of blackberries for scrummy pies.

Walk the remotest canal in Britain

Canals are meant to start and end somewhere purposeful, so few can claim to be remote in their entirety; but these manmade routes stray into Britain's deepest countryside where you call as loud as you want and only expect the sounds of wind and water to answer back. If solitude is your drug, head for towpaths as far away from car parks as you can find – and winter is the best time, at dawn or dusk. Many canals can feel remote only a mile or so out of town, but it's hard to beat the wilderness of stretches of the Caledonian, the Mon & Brec, the Macclesfield or the Caldon.

Walk one of the 7 Wonders

Why not explore the 7 Wonders of the Waterways on foot?

Walk in a group

Local canal societies often organise group walks, or why not join your local branch of the Ramblers Association?
www.ramblers.co.uk

Walks with wheels

The great thing about canal towpaths is that many are accessible for wheels too, and ramblers in wheelchairs can access many of them easily. And kids love walks that mean they can take their bikes too! Good wheel-friendly canals with flat hard surfacing include the Kennet & Avon from Bath to Bristol, the Regent's Canal in London, Exeter Ship Canal.
www.waterscape.com

Walk to the pub

There's no shortage of characterful pubs along the waterways. Pubs played a huge part in the lives of traditional working boaters of the 17th & 18th centuries. And now, they make a great stop-off for boaters, cyclists and walkers, dotted along almost every canal mile.

Walk with a tent on your back

Stay at a waterside campsite. Or go wild camping – farmers are often happy to let you pitch your tent in fields bordering the canals as long as you ask in advance and respect the environment. In Scotland, wild camping is usually allowed.
Use our canalside campsite directory
www.coolcanalsguides.com

Walk with your hotel

Let a hotel boat carry your luggage while you enjoy a towpath walk during the day. Then onboard after dusk, someone else makes dinner and does the washing-up!
www.coolcanalsguides.com

Walk through a tunnel

If you don't mind walls dripping with spiders, sleeping bats and spooky ghost tales, towpaths run through most of the short tunnels (and even some of the longer ones!)

Walk with a dog

If you haven't already got a four-legged friend, why not rescue a homeless dog and gain a happy walking partner?
www.dogstrust.org.uk www.rspca.org.uk

Walk in all seasons

In spring, the canals burst with nature coming to life... and autumn is beautiful with its changing colours. Walk in summer when the canals are busy with boats, or go in winter to get the place to yourself.

Start Canalbagging

There are people who scramble up and down the 283 Scottish Munros, ticking them off a list one by one; and others who aim to trek all 214 Wainwright fells. Then there's folk who go island bagging and Marilyn bagging. Could canalbagging be a new addiction? Want to join in?
www.canalbagging.com

NOTICE.
This
BRIDGE
Is insufficient to carry a
HEAVY MOTOR CAR
The Registered Axle Weight of any axle of which exceeds

TONS
or the Registered Axle-Weights of the several
axles of which exceed in the aggregate

TONS
or a Heavy Motor Car drawing a
TRAILER
if the Registered Axle-Weights of the several Axles
of the HEAVY MOTOR CAR and the
Axle-Weights of the several Axles of the
TRAILER
Exceed in the aggregate

GREAT WESTERN RAILWAY CO
PADDINGTON STATION
LONDON

AT THIS SPOT IN 1946

ON BOARD 'CRESSY'
TOM & ANGELA ROLT
FIRST MET
ROBERT AICKMAN
AND DECIDED TO FOUND THE
INLAND WATERWAYS ASSOC.

ERECTED   BY THE

WORC— B'HAM CANAL SOCIETY

THE
PLAQUE
WAS UNVEILED ON
AUGUST 13TH 2006
BY
SONIA ROLT
IT COMMEMORATES THE SIXTIETH ANNIVERSARY
OF THE IWA MEETING DESCRIBED ABOVE AND
THE START OF THE DIAMOND JUBILEE CELEBRATIONS OF
THE INLAND WATERWAYS ASSOCIATION
AND IT CORRECTS THE DATE GIVEN IN ERROR
BY ROBERT AICKMAN HIMSELF IN 1969
BEFORE THE ABOVE PLAQUE WAS ERECTED

IWA WEST MIDLANDS REGION
THE WORCESTER BIRMINGHAM
CANAL SOCIETY

The 7 Wonders of the Waterways

Robert Aickman, founder of the Inland Waterways' Association (IWA), drew up a list over fifty years ago of some of the most amazing canal engineering feats:

Pontcysyllte Aqueduct

See narrowboats fly through the sky on the UK's highest aqueduct, 127ft above the River Dee.
Details: Pontcysyllte Aqueduct
Location: Trevor Basin
Llangollen Canal OS SJ270420
Further info: A World Heritage Site.

Standedge Tunnel

3¼ mile-long tunnel through the Pennines, as if they weren't in the way at all.
Details: Standedge Tunnel & Visitor Centre
T:01484 844298 www.standedge.co.uk
Location: Marsden
Huddersfield Narrow Canal OS SE040120
Further info: Open April-Oct. Visitor Centre with café, guided & through boat trips.

Burnley Embankment

The 'straight mile' carries the canal over the rooftops of Burnley, near the Weavers' Triangle.
Details: Burnley Embankment
Location: Burnley
Leeds & Liverpool Canal OS SD844325
Further info: Almost a mile long and up to 60ft high in places.

Barton Swing Aqueduct

A canal full of water amazingly swings out of the way for ships on the canal below.
Details: Barton Swing Aqueduct
Carries the Bridgewater Canal over the Manchester Ship Canal.
Location: Barton upon Irwell
Bridgewater Canal OS SJ767976
Further info: Operates all year.

Bingley 5 Rise

Unique 5-lock staircase to heaven carries the canal up 60ft above Bingley's mills.
Details: Bingley Five Rise
T:0113 2816860
Location: Bingley
Leeds & Liverpool Canal OS SE107399
Further info: Boat passage through flight Mon-Fri needs to be booked.

Caen Hill Flight

16 wide locks pounded closely together take boats miraculously up and down hill.
Details: Caen Hill Flight
Location: Devizes.
Kennet & Avon Canal OS ST983614
Further info: The highlight of 29 locks in the 2¼ miles leading to Devizes.

Anderton Boat Lift

The 'cathedral' of the canals lifts boats from the Trent & Mersey Canal to the Weaver.
Details: Anderton Boat Lift
T:01606 786777 www.andertonboatlift.co.uk
Location: Anderton, Northwich. Trent & Mersey Canal/Weaver Nav OS SJ647753
Further info: Visitor Centre open from February, boat lift and river trips Mar-Oct.

The Falkirk Wheel

(Not in the original list - a new 8th wonder?) Opened in 2002. An incredible engineering marvel, world's first & only rotating boat lift.
Details: Falkirk Wheel
T:08700 500208 www.thefalkirkwheel.co.uk
Location: Falkirk
Union/Forth & Clyde Canals OS NS852801
Further info: Lifts boats 115ft.

Waterways Who's Who

The great engineers

James Brindley (1716-1772)
Pioneering genius responsible for the first canals and for developing the concept of canal networks.

John Rennie (1761-1821)
Famous for bridges and canal engineering, such as the Dundas Aqueduct on the Kennet & Avon Canal.

Thomas Telford (1757-1834)
Prolific engineer responsible for marvels such as Pontcysyllte Aqueduct (now a World Heritage Site) and the second Harecastle Tunnel.

The great entrepreneurs

Josiah Wedgwood (1730-1795)
Founder of Wedgwood pottery, he was quick to support canal development and collaborated with Brindley on the Trent & Mersey Canal. When complete, he was able to use the canal to transport clay to his factories and finished goods to the ports.

John Cadbury (1801-1889)
One of many Quaker social reformers and businessmen who supported the canals. Cocoa beans were carried by waterway from Bristol docks to Birmingham to the famous Cadbury's chocolate factories.

Sir Titus Salt (1803-1876)
Wool baron who created Saltaire village (a World Heritage Site) for his mill workers on the Leeds & Liverpool Canal. Similar to Bournville village, built by John Cadbury's son for workers in Birmingham, both had a distinct absence of pubs due to their Quaker influence until a bar 'Don't Tell Titus' opened at Saltaire in 2007.

And today...

British Waterways (BW)
Responsible for over 2,200 miles of Britain's canals and rivers.
www.british-waterways.co.uk

Waterscape
BW's official leisure guide to canals, rivers and lakes. www.waterscape.com

Inland Waterways' Association (IWA)
Founded by Thomas Rolt and Robert Aickman in 1946. Rolt fought ceaselessly to keep the waterways open for his narrowboat Cressy and for future generations of boaters - and the work carries on vigorously today.
www.waterways.org.uk

Waterway Recovery Group (WRG)
Voluntary organisation, running work camps to help restore derelict canals.
www.wrg.org.uk

National Waterways Museums
One museum in three locations - Ellesmere Port, Gloucester and Stoke Bruerne. The museums have interactive displays, the largest collection of historic boats in the world and a Waterways Archive preserving artefacts of canal history back to the 1700s.
www.nwm.org.uk

The Canal Trusts and Societies
Tackling restoration and management of the inland waterways. Most canals have an active Trust or Society with regular events, meetings, talks and fundraising.
Why not join your local canal society?

The Waterways Trust
National charity promoting greater public enjoyment of the inland waterways.
www.thewaterwaystrust.co.uk

Useful info

Waterways

British Waterways
www.britishwaterways.co.uk

Waterscape
www.waterscape.com

The Waterways Trust
www.thewaterwaystrust.org.uk

Inland Waterways Association (IWA)
www.waterways.org.uk

Waterway Recovery Group
www.wrg.org.uk

The Horseboating Society
www.horseboatingsociety.co.uk

Tourist Boards

Visit Britain
www.visitbritain.com

Enjoy England
www.enjoyengland.com

Visit Scotland
www.visitscotland.com

Visit Wales
www.visitwales.com

Waterways publications

Waterways World
www.waterwaysworld.com

Canal Boat
www.canalboat.co.uk

Towpath Talk
www.towpathtalk.co.uk

Canals & Rivers
www.canalsandrivers.co.uk

Travel

Buses: **Traveline**
T:0871 2002233 www.traveline.org.uk

Trains: **National Rail Enquiries**
T:08457 484950 www.nationalrail.co.uk

Walking & outdoors

Ramblers' Association
Walking information and canal walks
www.ramblers.org.uk

Disabled Ramblers Organisation
www.disabledramblers.co.uk

Sustrans
www.sustrans.org.uk

National Trails
www.nationaltrail.co.uk

National disabled access register
www.directenquiries.com

Wildlife

The Wildlife Trusts
www.wildlifetrusts.org

British Waterways Wildlife Survey
www.waterscape.com

National Swan Sanctuary
www.theswansanctuary.org.uk

Heritage

National Waterways Museum
www.nwm.org.uk

London Canal Museum
www.canalmuseum.org.uk

Canal bloggers

Granny Buttons
www.grannybuttons.com

Glossary

The canal has its own lingo...

Aqueduct: structure carrying a canal over a road, railway or river

Arm: short stretch of canal branching off from the main canal

Barge: cargo-carrying boat which is 16ft wide or more

Beam: width of a boat

Bow: front of a boat

Broad canal: canal over 7ft 6in wide

BW: British Waterways

Butty: unpowered boat towed by another boat with an engine

Canalia: gifts and crafts related to canals

Cratch: triangular structure at bow of boat

Cruiser: pleasure boat usually made of wood or fibreglass

Cruiser stern: extended external space at rear end of a narrowboat

Cut: slang for canal

Dolly: post used to tie mooring ropes round

Fender: externally hung bumper, usually made of rope, to protect hull of boat

Flight: series of locks close together

Gongoozler: Boaters' lingo describing onlookers

Gunwales: (pronounced 'gunnels') ridge to walk on along sides of a boat

Idle Women: the cheeky nickname given to the women who worked on canal boats during World War II to help the war effort. The name came from the initials 'IW' on the Inland Waterways badges they wore.

IWA: Inland Waterways' Association

Junction: where two or more canals meet

Legging: lying on top of boat and using legs on walls to push boat through tunnel

Lock: a water-holding chamber with gates and paddles to lift boats up and down hills

Milepost: short posts informing boatmen about distances travelled

Narrowboat: canal boats which are no wider than 7ft

Narrow canal: canals built for boats up to 70ft long and 7ft wide

Navvies: nickname for the navigators who dug the canals

Port: left side of boat when facing the bow

Pound: stretch of level water between locks, whether a few feet or a few miles

Roses and Castles: traditional folk art

Scumble: painting technique simulating the appearance of wood grain

Silt: mud that builds up at bottom of canal

Starboard: right side of the boat when facing the bow

Staircase locks: locks close together without pounds in between

Stern: the rear of a boat

Tiller: steering wheel of a boat, shaped like a pole

Towpath: path alongside canal built for working horses pulling boats

Tug: boat that pulls another boat

Tupperware: humorously irreverent name narrowboaters give fibreglass boats

Waterscape: the leisure website for British Waterways

Wide beam narrowboat: boat that looks like a narrowboat but is wider than 7ft 6in

Windlass: hand tool used to wind lock paddles up and down

About Coolcanals Guides

How it all began...

It's one of those dreams to desert the norm, ditch the humdrum rush of daily life...escape to the freedom of living on the water in a boat. We did it and took our 4 cats with us. We got rid of the house, car, TV, washing machine... and swapped them for a simple eco life. We hand-built the interior of our narrowboat-home using free reclaimed wood and started a new off-grid lifestyle travelling Britain's inland waterways.

Living on a narrowboat means slowing down to canal time and enjoying the basic things in life. Gathering logs for the stove, boiling the kettle from rationed water, starting the day at first light and ending it with the night's stars. It's an outdoor lifestyle where most of the good things are free and 'make do and mend' isn't drudgery. Somehow priorities change.

About Coolcanals now...

The waterways have taken us to all sorts of extremes and our travels carry on... by boat, bike and boot. We think we know some of the waterways best-kept secrets and enjoy creating books about some of the things we love the most.